HOW TO TAKE
GOOD PICTURES

HOW TO TAKE GOOD PICTURES

A PHOTO GUIDE BY Kodak

The world's best-selling photography book
Over 400 photos and the latest on KODAK Films

Ballantine Books • New York

HOW TO TAKE
GOOD PICTURES

Copyright © 1981, 1982, 1987, 1988, 1990
by Eastman Kodak Company
Eastman Kodak Company, Author

All rights reserved under International and Pan-American Copyright Conventions. No part of this publication may be reproduced, stored in a retrieval system, or transmitted, in any form, or by any means, electronic, mechanical, photocopying, recording, or otherwise, without the prior written permission of the copyright owner. Published in the United States by Ballantine Books, a division of Random House, Inc., New York, and simultaneously in Canada by Random House of Canada, Limited, Toronto, Canada.

Library of Congress Catalog Number: 89-90935
ISBN 0-345-36553-4

Manufactured in the United States of America
36th Edition (Revised), 1990 Printing

9 8 7 6 5 4 3

Contents

INTRODUCTION

Photography offers a twofold thrill to picture-takers. There's the delight in the event that you are planning to capture, and there's the pleasure in reviewing the pictures days, weeks, or even years later. With a little confidence in your knowledge, skill, and experience, you'll find that arranging or discovering a photographic scene provides great satisfaction. Pictures are reminders, keys to the past—even bits of history, personal or documentary. They also express your moods, impressions, and feelings of the moment— visible statements of a very personal art.

How to Take Good Pictures will help you to improve your pictures with any kind of camera. The advice on the following pages will familiarize you with many basic elements and techniques of photography. And as you become better acquainted with the principles of successful picture-taking, you'll feel more confident in the results.

How to Take Good Pictures gives instruction with pictures, rather than with columns of number- and formula-laden text. In this step-by-step primer, words serve to emphasize or clarify the messages offered by the illustrations. The book begins with basic ideas for picture improvement and moves on to advanced concepts. Start with the Top Ten Techniques for Better Pictures on the next 8 pages. Then, either read on in sequence or turn to those sections that interest you the most.

Keeping a ready camera and searching for the best viewpoint can pay rich rewards, as in this view of Mont St. Michel. Notice how the peaceful grazing sheep help to establish distance relationships. Muted light from cloudy skies gives a special mood.

THE TOP TEN TECHNIQUES FOR BETTER PICTURES

(If you read no further, following these ideas will improve your picture-taking dramatically.)

1

Move close to your subject. Whether it is a New England church or your daughter's high school prom, get close enough so that you see only the most important elements in the viewfinder. Failure to observe this simple guideline accounts for more unsuccessful pictures than any other photo mistake.

2

Make sure that your automatic or adjustable camera is set to give correct exposure. If your pictures are too light or too dark, check the camera manual and the film instructions. On a manually operated camera, you must set the film speed, shutter speed, and aperture. Many automatic cameras set these controls automatically.

Correct exposure

Overexposure

Underexposure

3

Carefully observe both background and foreground in your viewfinder before you take the picture. Clutter or confusing elements detract from the main subject. Keep your pictures as simple as possible.

Cluttered background   *Simple background*

4

You must make flash pictures within the flash-to-subject distance range for correct exposure with snapshot cameras. For automatic or manually adjustable cameras, the distance determines any adjustments to be made.

Flash is for dark places.

5

Hold your camera steady. Shaky hands or pushing the shutter-release button too abruptly may give you fuzzy pictures. Brace the camera with both hands against your forehead and gently press the shutter-release button.

Steady camera, sharp pictures

Shaky camera, fuzzy pictures

6

Become thoroughly familiar with your camera. Read the camera manual carefully so that you'll be comfortable making adjustments under a wide variety of conditions. As you read the manual, keep your camera in hand for reference.

Read your camera manual thoroughly.

7

Place your subject slightly off-center. When shown dead-center in a picture, your subject may appear static and rather dull. Experiment to see where different subjects look best. Some cameras take square pictures and others take rectangular ones. If your camera takes rectangular pictures, you can get both horizontal and vertical pictures by turning the camera.

Try placing your subject off center.

8

Rather than posing people in a starchy, uncomfortable manner, engage them in a natural, absorbing activity to take their eyes off you and the camera. When people are doing something familiar, their bodies and faces will relax. The couple below was posed, of course, but the picture-taker found a way to draw their attention and commemorate a holiday at the same time.

Keep people occupied.

9

Watch the direction of light in your scene. People usually squint in bright, direct light and the dark shadows are often unattractive. Light from the side or from behind your subject may be more effective than light from the front. Picture-taking in the shade or on an overcast day may be better, too, if it is possible with your camera.

Frontlighting—light from the front

Backlighting—light from behind

Bright, direct light

Overcast day

10

Take plenty of pictures. Every professional knows that the potential for success increases when more pictures are taken. Think about some of the rare scenes you'll encounter; film is far less expensive than a missed opportunity.

ABOUT YOUR CAMERA

TYPES OF CAMERAS

All cameras provide the same function—to allow a specific quantity of light to strike film. In simple terms, the light makes an image on the film and you get a picture. When you make pictures on a black-and-white, color negative, or color slide film, the film is usually processed by a photofinisher. A slide film provides color slides, and a black-and-white or color print film provides prints and negatives.

In this book, we'll discuss the use of simple cartridge-loading cameras and 35 mm cameras that accept film magazines. These cameras all work in basically the same way. Their designs may be slightly different, but the controls perform similar functions. In the next few pages, we'll provide a thumbnail sketch of each camera type, including its features and its operating procedures. Since some cameras are more complex than others, we'll devote more space to them.

We'll be showing and describing some current cameras in this section. No matter what camera you have, you'll want to refer to the camera manual for specific information on loading and operating procedures. Kodak can furnish a replacement manual for a recent Kodak camera if your manual has disappeared. The same may be true with other manufacturers. Try your photo dealer if information for your camera is unavailable. Dealers are familiar with many cameras and should be happy to help.

CARTRIDGE-LOADING CAMERAS

Cartridge-loading cameras are easy to use. They come in two sizes: 110 and 126. Loading film into them is simple. Most of the camera adjustments are automatic, so there are no decisions to make during picture-taking.

Other Advantages. They are small and lightweight. You can easily slip a 110 camera into your pocket or purse and not feel weighed down by heavy, cumbersome equipment. Picture-taking can be spontaneous and fun. Some photographers who typically use more advanced cameras also carry a cartridge-loading camera for making snapshots.

Cameras designed for 110 and 126 cartridges are lightweight and easy to use. The KODAK EKTRALITE 10 and KODAK INSTAMATIC X-15F Cameras are pictured here.

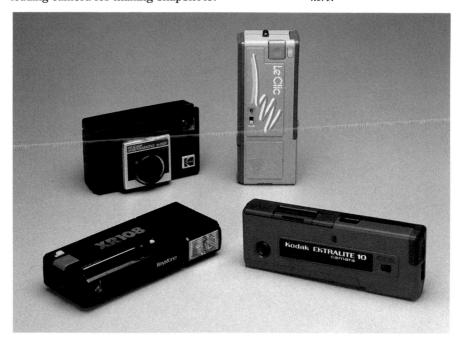

17

The simplest cartridge-loading cameras are also the easiest to use. You just have to load the film and snap a picture. You can make pictures on sunny or hazy days outdoors, or under dim light with flash.

More advanced cartridge-loading cameras, which naturally cost more, may adapt to a wider range of lighting conditions. Not only can you take pictures in bright light, you can also take pictures on heavy, overcast days or in the shade. Some cameras even allow you to take pictures using high-speed film indoors without flash under typical household lighting.

Operation. Picture-taking with a cartridge-loading camera is easy and fun. Loading is the first step. Let's take a look.

The small 110 cartridge fits in 110 cameras such as the EKTRALITE 10 Camera, and the larger 126 cartridge fits in the familiar INSTAMATIC X-15F Camera.

Loading

1. Insert the cartridge—it fits only one way. Close the film-compartment door

2. Push the film advance until it locks into place. (You may have to press the shutter-release button first.)

3. Number "1" will appear in the window—you're ready to take pictures.

Unloading

1. When you see a fully exposed cartridge in the window of a 110 or 126 camera, it's time to unload.

2. Depress the latch and open the film-compartment door.

3. Remove the cartridge and have the film processed.

CAMERAS FOR SPECIAL USES

You may want to consider other cameras for special purposes, such as single-use cameras. The KODAK FLING 35 Camera is an easy-to-use camera for taking pictures outdoors under bright sunlight to partly cloudy conditions. The FLING 35 Camera comes with film already inside. After exposing your last picture, return the entire camera with film inside to your photo dealer for processing. You'll receive finished prints, but the camera will not be returned.

The KODAK STRETCH 35 Camera is a single-use camera that features a 25 mm wide-angle lens for making panoramic pictures. The 12-exposure roll of 35 mm KODACOLOR GOLD 200 Film is already loaded in the camera at the time of purchase.

The KODAK FLING 35 Camera is for single use.

The KODAK STRETCH 35 Camera is a single-use camera that captures panoramic scenes.

All-weather cameras are useful when you go to the beach, white-water rafting, or skiing, and you don't want to risk exposing your camera to the harsh elements. You can also use all-weather cameras in the rain or the snow. You can even drop the KODAK EXPLORER Camera in the water; it floats!

Another Kodak camera is both all-weather and single-use—the KODAK WEEKEND 35 Camera. In addition, you can take the camera underwater.

You can use the KODAK EXPLORER Camera in harsh weather conditions.

35 mm CAMERAS

There are dozens of 35 mm cameras on the market today. They range from simple point-and-shoot cameras to advanced single-lens-reflex (SLR) models with interchangeable lenses and programmable modes. The type you choose will depend largely on your budget and how involved you want to be in picture-taking. Many people start with a smaller, less expensive camera and then, as their techniques become more advanced, they progress to a model that offers more options. Others choose to stay with an easier-to-use compact camera because of its convenience.

KODAK CAMERAS

Kodak offers a full line of automatic 35 mm cameras. To help you get great pictures, some of the KODAK Cameras feature automatic film advance and rewind, a focus-free lens, automatic film-speed setting, and a flash-fill and flash-defeat feature on the more advanced models. Choose the camera that's best for you according to your needs and your budget.

KODAK Cameras have many automatic features, making them convenient and easy to use.

OPERATING COMPACT 35 mm CAMERAS

Here's an overview of how to load a compact 35 mm camera. Review the instructions for your camera to see how they may differ. Some cameras require you to set the film speed. On advanced models, automatic loading, advancing, and rewinding of the film means there is no fumbling in the middle of the action.

1. Slide the film-compartment latch in the direction of the arrow to open the film-compartment door.

3. Pull the film leader towards the take-up spool. Align the end of the film with the film load mark and make sure the film perforations engage with the sprocket teeth.

2. Insert the film magazine into the film chamber. Check the film-loading diagram in the film chamber for proper position of the film magazine.

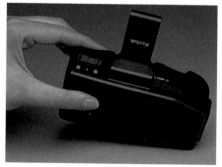

4. Close the film-compartment door. The camera automatically advances the film and the exposure counter to "1." You're ready to make pictures.

Loading a 35 mm SLR Camera

Open the back cover by pushing down on the back cover latch.

Insert a film magazine into the film compartment. The edge of the leader strip with the sprocket holes should be at the bottom.

Close the back cover.

The film and film counter will advance to number 1 with some automatic cameras. With others you must advance the film manually. You are now ready for picture-taking.

Unloading a 35 mm SLR Camera

When you have reached the end of the film and it will not advance further, it is time to unload. The film counter will indicate that you are at the end.

Activate the automatic rewind if your camera has one, or rewind it manually, if necessary. Then open the camera back and remove the film.

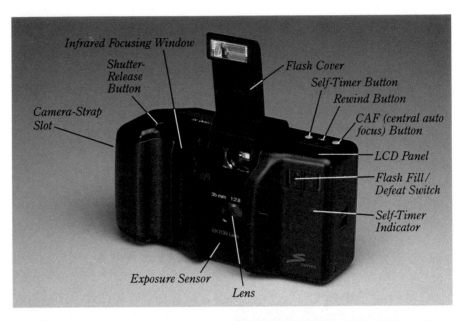

Infrared Focusing Window

Shutter-Release Button

Flash Cover

Self-Timer Button

Rewind Button

CAF (central auto focus) Button

Camera-Strap Slot

LCD Panel

Flash Fill/ Defeat Switch

Self-Timer Indicator

Exposure Sensor

Lens

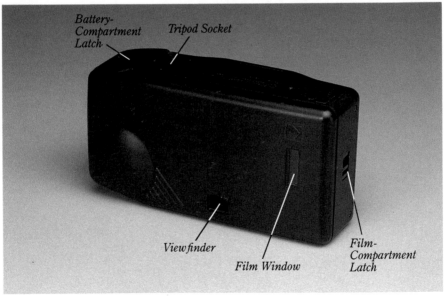

Battery-Compartment Latch

Tripod Socket

Viewfinder

Film Window

Film-Compartment Latch

AUTOMATIC FOCUS

Most compact and SLR 35 mm cameras today focus automatically. One camera can even use its autofocus system to compose the scene by adjusting the built-in zoom lens. You simply center your subject in the viewfinder, within the autofocus frame marks. Gently press the shutter release halfway to lock in the focus. Then recompose the picture, if desired. Continue to press the shutter release the rest of the way to take the picture.

Advanced 35 mm SLR cameras allow you to choose from two or three autofocus modes and a manual focus mode. You can choose a single-shot focus mode for still subjects. As with the compact cameras, you position your subject within the viewfinder, press the shutter release halfway to lock in the focus, recompose the scene, and press the shutter release fully. Or, you can select a continuous focus mode that refocuses as a subject moves. You might choose manual focus when you want to carefully position the range of sharpness (depth of field).

Single-Lens-Reflex Cameras. Fully automatic single-lens-reflex (SLR) 35 mm cameras are popular with today's photographers. DX-encoded films have made automatic film-speed setting possible. Automatic film advance and rewind, autofocus, and automatic exposure make these cameras almost as easy to use as snapshot cameras. However, SLRs have additional features, such as a variety of interchangeable lenses, accessory flash units, and additional exposure modes that make them more versatile.

You can choose an exposure mode appropriate for the subject you are photographing and the results you want. The common modes include manual, program, shutter-speed-preferred, and aperture-preferred. A camera that offers several of these modes is known as a multi-mode camera. We explain these modes in more detail on the following pages. And, of course, SLR means that you compose the scene through the same lens that takes the picture. That means you get exactly what you see.

If you buy a multi-mode SLR camera and a few lenses, you will have to make decisions during picture-taking. You'll need to know when to choose one lens or one setting over another. You may not understand fully at first, but you will learn as you gain experience. These options allow you to get better results over a broader range of picture-taking conditions and allow you to be more creative.

There are dozens of 35 mm cameras to choose from. Pictured here are just a few.

Program Exposure. If your camera has one or several program modes, it means the camera can set both the shutter speed and the aperture after it meters the scene. Some cameras have only a "normal" program mode that does not give a preference to either aperture or shutter speed. Other cameras have additional programs designed for photographing action or scenes that require great depth of field (front-to-back sharpness). The program for photographing action is typically called an action program. The program for great depth of field is often called a depth program.

If you are photographing your son heading a soccer ball into the goal, set the camera on the action program. It favors a fast shutter speed and a moderate-to-large aperture; a typical setting might be **1/500 second** at *f*/4. But if you are photographing a field of daisies leading up to a barn, you'll need great depth of field—not a fast shutter speed. So set your camera to the depth program. It favors a small aperture and a moderate shutter speed; a typical setting might be 1/60 second at ***f*/11**. And if you are doing general photography, set your camera for the normal program; a typical setting might be 1/125 second at *f*/8.

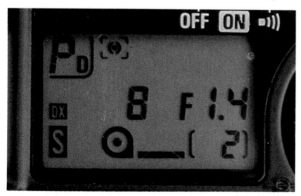

The "P" in the upper left corner of the camera display indicates it is set for program exposure; the "D" indicates it is the "depth" program.

Semi-automatic Modes

Shutter-Speed-Preferred. If your camera has a shutter-speed-preferred mode, you choose the shutter speed and the camera chooses the aperture. Some cameras with program exposure also have semi-automatic modes. The difference between this mode and the program mode is that, with shutter-speed-preferred, you select the shutter speed and it stays constant (until you choose to change it). If you focus on a new scene, the old shutter speed is still in effect. You would need to rethink your needs, and change the shutter speed manually, if necessary.

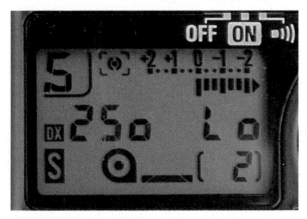

When the camera is in the shutter-speed-preferred mode, you set the shutter speed; the camera sets the aperture for the lighting conditions.

Aperture-Preferred. If your camera has an aperture-preferred mode, you choose the aperture and the camera chooses the shutter speed. In dim light, keep in mind that you would usually want to select a larger aperture. Otherwise, the camera may set a slow shutter speed that would require use of a tripod. (The larger the aperture, the smaller the *f*-stop number.) In brightly lit scenes, use a small aperture.

When the camera is in the aperture-preferred mode, you set the aperture; the camera sets the shutter speed for the lighting conditions. A good aperture for general picture-taking is f/8.

Manual Cameras. Although several automatic cameras have a manual mode, only a few cameras on the market today are solely manual. With manual cameras or an automatic camera in the manual mode, you have to set both the shutter speed and the aperture. The majority of manual cameras have built-in exposure meters that help you make appropriate settings for the lighting conditions and for the film you're using. Even if your camera does not offer manual exposure, it's helpful to understand the reasons for choosing particular apertures or shutter speeds. This information can be valuable when deciding which mode to choose on automatic cameras.

Many cameras give you exposure information in the viewfinder. You may see the shutter speed and the aperture settings, and sometimes a bracket with a needle that points to + or − for over- or under-exposure. Older cameras may have a bracket with a needle on the outside of the camera. Some of the latest cameras have a liquid crystal display atop the camera that gives exposure information.

Some older manual cameras do not have a built-in meter, and you must use a handheld meter to determine your camera settings. Also, unlike the newer cameras with the autofocus feature, you must focus the camera to take a picture. Since focusing varies from camera to camera, it's best to consult your instruction manual for more details. In addition, with manual cameras, you must set the film-speed dial manually for the speed of the film you are using.

WHAT'S NEW

In addition to focusing modes, other new features to look for on many advanced 35 mm cameras are push button controls with liquid crystal displays. Shutter-speed dials and aperture rings have disappeared from many cameras. Now you press a combination of buttons to select exposure modes, exposure compensation, fill flash and so on. Some SLRs use a segmented metering system that measures light in several areas of the scene. Then it compares the reading to thousands of similar scenes stored in its computer memory, and it chooses the appropriate aperture and shutter speed. Such a system gives you good results under backlit conditions and other scenes filled with large areas of light and dark.

Other advances have been in the area of zoom lenses. A wide-range zoom lens such as a 35 to 200 mm lens is quite versatile. With a wide range of focal lengths built into one lens, you no longer have to carry a collection of lenses. At the 35 mm setting, you can include an entire race track. At the 200 mm setting, you can fill the picture with a car careening around a curve. Not only does it make your camera bag lighter weight, but it means you no longer have to fumble with changing lenses in the middle of picture-taking.

A sophisticated point-and-shoot camera known as a "bridge" camera has many of the same features as a traditional SLR camera, along with a built-in auto-focus zoom lens. There are choices for action mode, object mode, and exposure compensation. Although the bridge camera is bulkier than most cameras, its many features make it almost as versatile as an SLR camera.

Shown here are two manufacturer's versions of bridge cameras.

Outdoor Daylight Settings for a Manual Camera

Film Speed ISO	Light Conditions				
	Bright or Hazy Sun on Light Sand or Snow	Bright or Hazy Sun (Distinct Shadows)	Weak Hazy Sun (Soft Shadows)	Cloudy Bright (No Shadows)	Open Shade or Heavy Overcast
25–32	**1/125, f/11** 1/60, f/16 1/30, f/22 1/250, f/8 1/500, f/5.6 1/1000, f/4	**1/125, f/8** 1/60, f/11 1/30, f/16 1/250, f/5.6 1/500, f/4 1/1000, f/2.8	**1/125, f/5.6** 1/60, f/8 1/30, f/11 1/250, f/4 1/500, f/2.8 1/1000, f/2	**1/125, f/4** 1/60, f/5.6 1/30, f/8 1/250, f/2.8 1/500, f/2 1/1000, f/1.4	**1/60, f/4** 1/30, f/5.6 1/125, f/2.8 1/250, f/2 1/500, f/1.4
64 100*– color negative	**1/125, f/16** 1/60, f/22 1/250, f/11 1/500, f/8 1/1000, f/5.6	**1/125, f/11** 1/60, f/16 1/30, f/22 1/250, f/8 1/500, f/5.6 1/1000, f/4	**1/125, f/8** 1/60, f/11 1/30, f/16 1/250, f/5.6 1/500, f/4 1/1000, f/2.8	**1/125, f/5.6** 1/60, f/8 1/30, f/11 1/250, f/4 1/500, f/2.8 1/1000, f/2	**1/125, f/4** 1/60, f/5.6 1/30, f/8 1/250, f/2.8 1/500, f/2 1/1000, f/1.4
125 200*– color negative	**1/250, f/16** 1/125, f/22 1/500, f/11 1/1000, f/8	**1/250, f/11** 1/60, f/22 1/125, f/16 1/500, f/8 1/1000, f/5.6	**1/125, f/11** 1/60, f/16 1/30, f/22 1/250, f/8 1/500, f/5.6 1/1000, f/4	**1/125, f/8** 1/60, f/11 1/30, f/16 1/250, f/5.6 1/500, f/4 1/1000, f/2.8	**1/125, f/5.6** 1/60, f/8 1/30, f/11 1/250, f/4 1/500, f/2.8 1/1000, f/2
200 400*– color negative	**1/500, f/16** 1/250, f/22 1/1000, f/11	**1/500, f/11** 1/125, f/22 1/250, f/16 1/1000, f/8	**1/250, f/11** 1/125, f/16 1/60, f/22 1/500, f/8 1/1000, f/5.6	**1/250, f/8** 1/125, f/11 1/60, f/16 1/30, f/22 1/500, f/5.6 1/1000, f/4	**1/250, f/5.6** 1/125, f/8 1/60, f/11 1/30, f/16 1/500, f/4 1/1000, f/2.8
400	**1/1000, f/16** 1/500, f/22	**1/500, f/16** 1/250, f/22 1/1000, f/11	**1/500, f/11** 1/250, f/16 1/125, f/22 1/1000, f/8	**1/500, f/8** 1/250, f/11 1/125, f/16 1/60, f/22 1/1000, f/5.6	**1/500, f/5.6** 1/250, f/8 1/125, f/11 1/60, f/16 1/30, f/22 1/1000, f/4
1000– color negative	**1/1000, f/22**	**1/1000, f/16** 1/500, f/22	**1/1000, f/11** 1/500, f/16 1/250, f/22	**1/1000, f/8** 1/500, f/11 1/250, f/16 1/125, f/22	**1/1000, f/5.6** 1/500, f/8 1/250, f/11 1/125, f/16 1/60, f/22

Note: Shutter speeds are in seconds. Exposure settings in heavy type indicate suggested settings for general use.

*Since these color negative films tolerate moderate overexposure, the values in the table above are designed for maximum exposure latitude. Slide films, however, must be exposed accurately.

AUTOMATIC SETTING OF FILM SPEED

Most Kodak 35 mm film magazines are DX-encoded. Nearly all SLR cameras and many compact cameras read this code and automatically set the camera's metering system accordingly. Now you don't have to worry about getting poor pictures because you forgot to change the film-speed setting when you changed film. Choose film with appropriate speed based on picture-taking conditions. When you take pictures under normal daylight conditions or indoors with flash, you may want to choose a film with a speed of ISO 100 or 200; for low-light level conditions, you may want to use a film with a speed of ISO 400, 1000, or 1600.

REWINDING THE FILM

Rewind the film after you take the last picture. Some cameras automatically rewind the film when you reach its end. With others, you press a rewind switch or turn a crank. Do not open the back door until after you rewind the film, or your film will be fogged.

FLASH

Electronic flash is the most common source of sup-
plemental lighting for 35 mm cameras. It is compact
and convenient to carry. It allows you to take pictures in low light to soften harsh shadows or to extend the depth of field in closeups.

Most compact cameras and many SLR cameras
have a small electronic flash built into the camera. On
some units the flash is stationary, while on others it is
extendible (either pops or flips up, or extends side-
ways). Opening the flash cover on the camera shown
extends the flash, turns on the power, and uncovers
the picture-taking lens. When the flash is charged,
you are ready to take a picture.

Occasionally, you will have to replace the camera
battery which powers the flash. You can tell it needs
replacing on some cameras by a weak-battery warn-
ing light; on other models you will know it needs
replacing when the flash takes longer to charge than
mentioned in the instruction manual.

This camera has a built-in flash as part of the lens cover that flips up for use.

Be sure to stay within the recommended flash range for the speed of the film you are using. If you are too close to the subject, your pictures may look too light; if you are beyond maximum distance, the flash loses its benefit and your pictures may appear dark. See your camera manual for the recommended flash range.

Older rangefinder cameras and many current single-lens-reflex (SLR) cameras have a shoe for holding auxiliary flash units. Simply slip the flash onto the shoe and make the connection with the PC cord (small cord supplied with the flash). On all recent SLR cameras, the shoe connects the flash electrically to the camera without the need for a PC cord. Be sure to set the camera's shutter speed as recommended by the camera instruction manual. Otherwise, the shutter may not be synchronized with the flash and you could obtain poor results.

Flash exposure made at the correct shutter speed.

Flash exposure made with camera set for too fast a shutter speed (not synchronized).

A fill-flash lever on some advanced models lets you use fill flash for backlit subjects, or to lighten shadows (especially on faces) in contrasty scenes. You simply slide in and hold the fill-flash lever while depressing the shutter-release button.

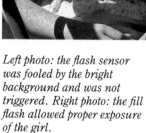

Left photo: the flash sensor was fooled by the bright background and was not triggered. Right photo: the fill flash allowed proper exposure of the girl.

Automatic Electronic Flash. When the light level is low, indoors or out, the built-in flash on many cameras will fire automatically. Check the manual for the exact flash range with your model camera. Generally, the maximum range is 15 to 20 feet, with the greater range for higher speed films.

Flash Exposure. Setting the aperture depends on the flash-to-subject distance. Generally, there are three systems—automatic, dedicated, and manual—for choosing the aperture. We'll discuss them in more detail in the "Flash" section of the book, page 152. Automatic flash units have a sensor that shuts off the flash when enough light has reached the subject. First, you set the film speed on the flash unit. Then you choose an aperture/distance-range mode and set the recommended aperture on the camera for that mode. Next, you set the flash-shutter speed, usually 1/60 or 1/125 second. Make sure that the subject is in the distance range for that flash mode, and then take the picture.

Automatic flash units require you to set the film speed on the calculator on the back of the flash unit and to choose an automatic flash mode based on the subject's distance from the flash. Here we chose the yellow mode and set the aperture—f/8 in this case— recommended by the flash unit. Make sure that the distance between flash and subject falls within the automatic flash range—1.6 to 8.5 feet in this case.

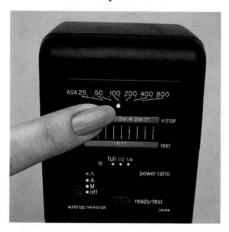

Dedicated flash systems differ, but the idea is generally the same. A sensor in the camera (not on the flash) determines when enough light has reached the film, and then shuts off the power in the flash unit. A camera with a dedicated flash will set the film speed, the aperture, and the shutter speed. You have only to stand within the distance range and take the picture. Most built-in flash units and many accessory units are dedicated. Since these systems vary, you'll want to pay careful attention to their instructions.

Most SLR cameras today have a hot shoe for attaching a flash unit without use of a PC cord.

Manual flash takes a few more steps. When the flash is connected to the camera, you set the film speed on the flash calculator, and focus on the subject. Refer to the distance scale on the lens barrel for the camera-to-subject distance. Then find that distance on the flash calculator. The aperture number will appear across from the distance. Set the lens aperture at that number and take a picture.

No matter the type of flash unit you use, wait until the ready-light glows to indicate the flash is charged before you take a picture. If you take a picture before the ready-light glows, your pictures may come out dark.

The flash-synch shutter speed for manual and automatic flash units is typically 1/60 or 1/125 second.

Set the recommended flash shutter speed on the camera. Then set the film speed on the flash calculator dial. Focus on your subject. The flash-to-subject distance will appear on the lens distance scale. Apply that distance to the flash calculator. Here it is 10 feet. The recommended aperture setting, here, between f/5.6 and f/8, will appear across from the flash-to-subject distance. Set the recommended aperture on the lens-aperture ring.

Electronic flash units work on either rechargeable batteries or disposable batteries. When the recycle times get longer than recommended by the flash manual, replace or recharge the batteries. For more important flash battery information, refer to page 157.

Note: *If the film-speed dial won't register the 1000-speed film you're using, set it to 500 and select a lens opening one stop smaller than indicated.*

CAMERA HANDLING

Proper camera handling may be one of the most important contributions to good pictures. These tips will help you improve the way you take pictures.

Holding the Camera Steady
Start taking sharp pictures by holding the camera steady. Stand comfortably balanced with your legs slightly apart, or lean against a tree, wall, or railing. Grip the camera, one hand on each side, and gently press your elbows to your side. If you've been exerting—walking up a mountain trail, for example—let your breathing resume a slow, steady pace before taking a picture.

Pressing the Shutter-Release Button
Slowly press the shutter-release button to take a picture. This will give you a better chance for sharp pictures and help you maintain good composition.

Keeping the Lens Clear
One common problem is arranging a beautiful scene in the viewfinder only to discover later that a finger, the camera strap, part of the camera case, or even the lens cap covered the lens while you took a picture. Make it a practice to clear the lens area of obstructions before taking the picture.

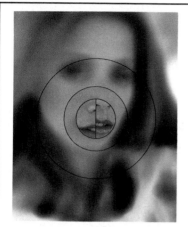

Focusing

The three common focusing systems are fixed focus, manual focus, and automatic focus. Fixed focus is common on simple cameras. With it you cannot adjust the focus. The camera maker sets the focus during manufacture to give sharp pictures over a specific range, typically four feet to infinity (great distance). As long as the subject is within the focus range, the photo will be sharp.

With manual focus, you have to adjust the lens each time you take a picture. For some older simple cameras, you set the lens to a distance symbol corresponding to the subject's approximate distance. The symbols may include a person's head and shoulders (close distance), a person's full figure (medium distance), and mountains (great distance). For other older simple cameras, instead of setting the lens to a symbol, you estimate the subject's distance and set it on a scale on the lens. A few cameras couple a rangefinder to the lens. To focus, you turn the lens-focusing ring until the two images in the center of the viewfinder coincide. Some SLR cameras still use manual focusing lenses. While looking through the camera's viewfinder, you turn a ring on the lens until the image is in focus. A typical SLR viewfinder includes optical focusing aids shown in the top photos.

Most of the advanced compact and SLR cameras have autofocusing, because it's so reliable and easy to use. You simply center the main subject in the viewfinder so that the autofocus system can focus on it and take the picture. If you don't want the subject centered in the actual picture, you can lock in the focus with the subject centered and then reframe the scene before you take the picture.

Using the Viewfinder

In some camera viewfinders, the picture area is defined by a bright rectangle or square. Other cameras use the entire viewfinder to frame the scene. Check your instruction manual to get the important elements of the scene into your picture.

When you see foreground litter or a confusing background in the viewfinder, choose another position. Horizons should be level.

Camera Support

Many automatic and adjustable cameras will operate at shutter speeds slower than 1/30 second. At these slow speeds, even your steadiest position, grip, and release may jiggle the camera and produce blurred pictures. For extra support, lean against a tree or wall or rest the camera on a table or rock. A tripod will give the most reliable support. A cable release will remove shaky hands from the camera.

Using the Self-Timer

The self-timer is handy when you want to include yourself in the picture. Set the timer, press the shutter-release button, and position yourself in the picture. You'll have about 10 seconds to get there. When you're arranging the picture in the viewfinder, leave room for yourself. Place your camera on a solid support such as a table, fence post, rock, or tripod.

FILM

Film is available in different sizes for different cameras. Check your camera manual for the correct film size. And choose film for the kind of pictures you want—color prints, color slides, or black-and-white prints.

Films also have different sensitivities to light. "Fast" films are very sensitive. You might use them in dim light. "Slower" films are good for very sharp pictures in bright light. You'll probably want to use a medium-speed film, such as KODACOLOR GOLD 200, for most picture-taking. Check your camera manual for the range of film speeds your camera can handle.

The speed or sensitivity of film is indicated by an ISO number. A medium-speed film might have an ISO rating of 64 to 200. High-speed film would be 250 to 640. Very high-speed films range from 800 to 1600, and a low-speed film 50 or less.

Most films are manufactured for taking pictures in daylight. Some slide and professional color negative films, however, are designed to give pictures with correct color balance when you use them with artificial light sources—household bulbs (tungsten) or photographic lamps. See pages 132 to 135 for more information on these films.

Film cartons carry a "Develop Before" date. Film, like food, can go bad from aging and may yield pictures of inferior quality. Check the date when you buy new film, and don't forget about film in your camera. Take the pictures and get them processed quickly. Film doesn't like extreme heat or humidity, either. Keep it out of direct sunlight and other hot spots.

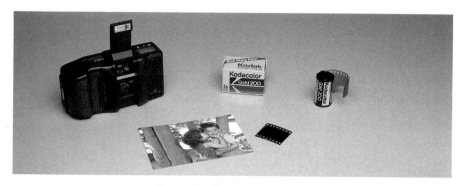

camera   print   *135 film box*   *negative*   *magazine*

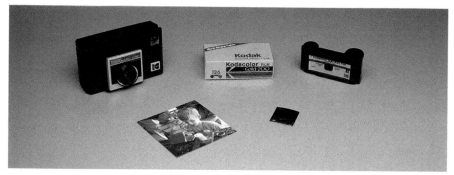

camera   print   *126 film box*   *negative*   *cartridge*

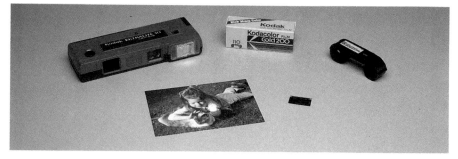

camera   print   *110 film box*   *negative*   *cartridge*

KODAK Film Choices

KODAK Films	Description	Sizes Available
for color prints		
KODACOLOR GOLD 100	Very high sharpness and extremely fine grain allow high degree of enlargement and wide exposure latitude. Excellent for use in general lighting conditions.	135
KODACOLOR GOLD 200	High sharpness and extremely fine grain, allows fast shutter speeds for capturing action or small apertures for increased depth of field under normal lighting conditions.	135, 110, 126
KODACOLOR GOLD 400	High-speed film for low-light situations without flash, allows fast shutter speeds or small apertures under normal lighting conditions. Medium sharpness and extremely fine grain offer good quality photographs.	135, 110
KODACOLOR GOLD 1600	Very high-speed film designed for low-light and fast-action situations. It is also an excellent choice for hand-held telephoto lenses, or for subjects that require good depth of field and high shutter speeds.	135
EKTAR 25	Kodak's sharpest and finest-grain color negative film. Use it to obtain outstanding enlargements. Good under very bright lighting conditions or indoors with flash. Use it only in a camera that can be set to ISO 25. Expose it carefully, since it has less latitude than KODACOLOR GOLD Films.	135
EKTAR 125	Micro-fine grain, extremely high sharpness, and very high resolving power. For use in daylight or with electronic flash, or under existing-light sources without filters.	135
EKTAR 1000	High speed, allows picture-taking under very low-light levels without flash, allows fast shutter speeds and small apertures under normal lighting conditions.	135

KODAK Films	Description	Sizes Available
for color slides		
KODACHROME 25 (Daylight)	Extremely fine grain, excellent color, high sharpness, use in bright sun or with electronic flash, or when slow shutter speeds or large lens openings are desired.	135
KODACHROME 64 (Daylight)	Medium-speed, general-purpose film. Exhibits remarkable sharpness and freedom from graininess.	135
KODACHROME 200 (Daylight)	Fine grain, higher speed, allows faster shutter speeds necessary when handholding longer lenses and for stopping action, smaller lens openings for greater depth of field, and use in low-light situations.	135
EKTACHROME 64 (Daylight)	General-purpose film with medium speed.	110
EKTACHROME 100 HC (Daylight)	Medium-speed film for general all-around use. It has sufficient speed to let you use higher shutter speeds or smaller lens openings in normal lighting. Excellent sharpness and graininess characteristics.	135
EKTACHROME 160 (Tungsten)	Medium-speed film for use with tungsten lamps and existing tungsten light. It has very fine grain and excellent sharpness. Can be push-processed to double the speed.	135
EKTACHROME 200 (Daylight)	Medium-speed film for existing light, fast action, subjects requiring good depth of field, and for extending the flash-distance range. It has very fine grain and excellent sharpness. Can be push-processed to double the speed.	135
EKTACHROME 400 (Daylight)	High-speed film for existing-light or low-light-level conditions, fast action, subjects requiring good depth of field, and for extending the flash-distance range. It has fine grain and good sharpness and can be push-processed to double the speed.	135
EKTACHROME P800/1600 Professional	Very high-speed film for existing light and fast action. This film exposed at EI 800 or EI 1600 provides good results in adverse lighting conditions. Can be push-processed as high as EI 3200.	135

PEOPLE

When you photograph people—friends and family or interesting strangers—you want them to look their best. Portray them naturally. Show some of the unique traits that distinguish them from the rest of the crowd. Spend a moment considering what important characteristics identify the people close to you. It might be helpful to suggest expressions, clothing, props, and activities that will encourage the real people to emerge from behind the snapshot smile-masks.

Direction of light

Frontlighting

Sidelighting

Backlighting

OUTDOORS

Light—its direction and intensity—is all-important in your outdoor portraits. Direct sunlight can illuminate a subject from one of three directions. *Frontlighting* is harsh, usually causing a person to squint, and often making heavy shadows on the person's face. *Sidelighting,* where half of the face is in shadow, can be effective for a dramatic portrayal. *Backlighting* will give a silhouette when the camera is adjusted for a sunlight exposure; it can give a gentle appearance, however, when the camera is adjusted to record the subject's most important features. (Backlighting can fool an automatic camera. See page 142.)

There are two ways to cope with direct, bright sunlight from any direction. One way is to place a piece of white cardboard in a position to reflect some light into the shadow areas of the subject. Almost anything in a light, neutral tone will do—white paper, white cardboard, white fabric, a newspaper, or a white wall.

Fill-in Flash. Fill-in flash can brighten dark shadows in outdoor pictures. A camera that has built-in flash or that takes disposable flash devices provides easy flash fill. Position your subject near the maximum distance recommended by the camera manual and take a flash picture.

Using Flash in Daylight

Some KODAK Cameras have a fill-flash feature. This can be used when the main subject has less light falling on it than the surrounding area. Without fill flash, the main subject would be underexposed. (This is because the automatic flash sensor is being fooled by the bright surroundings and is not triggered.) By sliding in and holding the fill-flash switch during picture-taking, you can overcome underexposure of the main subject.

If you have an adjustable or automatic camera that accepts an accessory flash, perform all the usual steps to take a flash picture (see pages 40-41) and 152-157). Set the camera for the sunlighted situation, but select a shutter speed that will synchronize with the flash—generally 1/60 or 1/125 second. A medium- or slow-speed film may be helpful. Then position your subject at a distance that will require more flash power than your flash unit can provide. You want the flash to fill the shadows subtly, not overpower the sunlight. See pages 160-161 for more on fill-in flash.

Overcast sky

From above

Direct sunlight

Another way is to use a flash unit on your camera to add a little brightness to the shadows. Photograph your subject from a distance where the flash provides a little less than half the light necessary for proper exposure. (See pages 160-161 for more information on flash-fill exposure.)

Light shade or overcast skies give more appealing pictures of people than direct sunlight. You'll get open, easy expressions without dark shadows. Since there's less light in these conditions, an automatic camera will automatically give more exposure. With a manual camera you'll have to make the necessary adjustments. (See pages 136-143.)

You can subtly change a person's appearance by changing the camera angle. A person photographed from above at a high camera angle seems smaller and less important than someone photographed from below at a low camera angle. When you aim the camera from eye level or a bit below, the effect is called normal. Most people prefer to be photographed at eye level. Be careful that an unusual camera angle doesn't distort your subject.

From below

At eye level

People have natural expressions when they're occupied.

Look through the viewfinder at the entire scene. Make sure that no clutter in the background or foreground interferes with your view of the subject. Move in close to the person—close enough to keep only the essential features in the picture. (If you're using fill-in flash, move in only as far as good exposure will permit.) Another way to keep the foreground and background simple is to change camera position and angle until you see exactly what you want in the viewfinder. You can control depth of field so that the person is sharp and the rest of the scene is blurred. (See page 144.)

People have natural expressions when they're comfortable. Try to have your subjects in relaxed positions—leaning against something or seated. When people have something to occupy their hands and attention, you'll get authentic portraits. Make sure your model is wearing clothing he or she finds appropriate and that appeals to your eye for color, coordination, and neatness.

Depth of field

Large aperture—f/3.5   *Small aperture—f/22*

Window light

Tungsten light

INDOORS

Most of the outdoor guidelines apply to making effective portraits indoors. You want people to be comfortable, relaxed, and to appear in pictures as they do in day-to-day life. Seated comfortably in a pleasant spot with an attractive, simple background is one answer. An alternative is to engage your subject in an activity that is interesting, familiar, and appropriate, such as a hobby or sport.

Again, lighting is important. You'll find four possible sources for indoor light: existing light from outdoors shining through a window or a door, artificial light given by tungsten or fluorescent bulbs, flash, and strong tungsten bulbs in reflectors called photolamps. (See next page.)

Flash

Window light reflected from book

Existing Light. The existing light* looks best, of course, whether it's from the outdoors or from artificial sources such as household lamps. If you use light from the outside, move your subject close to a window or doorway, positioned so that lighting on the face is even and so that your picture will not include much of the bright window or doorway. The bright area would fool an exposure meter of an automatic camera into underexposing the subject's face. A reflector can brighten the shadows caused by light from a single direction.

Taking pictures by household lamps require fast film (ISO 400 or greater), slow shutter speeds (1/60 second or less) and wide apertures (*f*/2.8 or larger) because normal home lighting is much darker than daylight. Pose people near bright light outdoors. Pose people near bright light sources, but don't in-

Using Photolamps

Create effective lighting with photolamps. Bulbs and reflectors are sold by photo, hardware, and electrical dealers. One lamp, reflecting off a wall, will give a pleasing portrait. Three lamps give many lighting possibilities. Using an exposure meter or an automatic camera should give good exposure.

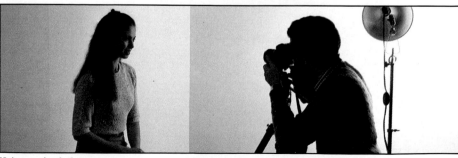

Using a single lamp

clude those lights in your picture. Try to have the lighting as even as possible on the person's face. When the lighting is extremely dim and you need a shutter speed slower than 1/30 second, mount your camera on a steady support such as a tripod for sharp pictures.

Tungsten bulbs give a different color light from daylight. Use high-speed film designed for tungsten light or use daylight film with an 80A filter attached to the camera lens†. In fluorescent light, also a different color from daylight, use daylight film and a CC30M filter†. Otherwise, your pictures may have a greenish tint. If you use any high-speed film for color prints, such as KODAK EKTAR 1000 or KODACOLOR GOLD 1600 Film, you can expect good results without a filter.

*See pages 162-165 for more on existing light.
†See pages 166-177 for more on filters.

Three lamps

Using An Exposure Meter. Many advanced automatic and adjustable cameras allow you to make some decisions about setting the camera for unusual lighting conditions. These cameras generally have a built-in exposure meter that either gives you advice on how to set the camera yourself or makes the adjustments for you. Older adjustable cameras may not have a built-in meter. If yours doesn't, you may know how to operate a handheld meter.

The best advice for using any meter, built-in or handheld, is to make a reading as close as possible to the subject, excluding the meter or camera shadow. Make your settings as the meter indicates from the close-up position. If the camera is automatic, there is usually some way to override the automatic setting feature in unusual exposure situations. Take a meter reading close to the subject and then back off to your preferred camera position. Adjust the camera manually to keep the exposure settings recommended by the meter at the close position. For better understanding of exposure, see pages 136-143. For better understanding of how your particular camera operates, check the instruction manual.

Flash. Flash, of course, is one of the most popular sources for light in dark places. Electronic flash units are available for most cameras, and the cost per flash is very low. Many units are automatic within certain distance ranges, allowing sufficient exposure without further adjustment. As with photolamps, a single flash will provide enough light, but it may be rather

Flash Pictures. Flash photography is easy with nearly any camera. Most snapshot cameras are equipped for an attachable flash device, such as a flip-flash or an accessory electronic flash unit or have a built-in electronic flash. Attach and/or turn on the flash device or unit; make sure that your subject is in the flash distance range, and make a picture. Allow the ready light on an electronic flash unit to glow before you make the next picture.

With 35 mm cameras that have built-in flash, you turn the flash on, focus the camera if necessary, and make a picture. Adjustable or automatic cameras that accept accessory flash units may require some adjustment. Some dedicated systems may need to have a particular aperture set on the camera. More sophisticated dedicated systems need no settings.

Automatic flash units operate in several distance ranges at different aperture settings, depending on film speed. Determine the typical distance you'll be photographing, and choose the appropriate mode on the flash unit. The unit usually requires a specific aperture setting for each flash mode.

With a manual flash, you set the film speed on the calculator on the back of the flash unit, then focus on the subject. Look at the lens-distance scale to find out the camera-to-subject distance. Refer to the flash-calculator dial and find the aperture to set on your camera—it will be approximately across from the camera-to-subject distance. There's a lot more to know about flash photography with automatic and adjustable cameras. See pages 152-161 for more information.

Using Flash
The most important guide for successful flash photography is to keep within the flash range. For snapshot cameras, the range might be 4 to 12 feet. With a more advanced flash, the range may vary. Check the instruction manuals for your camera and flash.

Direct flash

harsh. Bounce the flash off a light, neutral-color wall, ceiling, or white card for a softer light more suitable for portraiture. Flash exposure depends on flash-to-subject distance. For more information on flash exposure and bounce flash, refer to pages 154-159.

Bounced flash

Bounce Flash. Bouncing the flash off a ceiling or wall softens the harsh effect common to direct flash. It's easy with most cameras that accept accessory electronic-flash units.

Some sensor-automatic electronic flash units will function automatically when you tilt the flash head toward the bounce surface. The sensor must remain aimed at your subject. Use the automatic mode that required the largest lens aperture (smallest number), and stay well within the maximum flash range. Automatic units that have fixed heads must be used manually, as described below.

With a manual electronic flash unit or with one that has a fixed flash (non-tilting) head, you must remove the flash from the camera. You'll be able to connect the flash and camera with a special electrical cord (PC-cord), sold by photo dealers. Make settings as follows. Determine the approximate distance that the flash will travel—from flash to bounce surface to subject—and use that distance to find the corresponding lens aperture on the flash calculator. Increase the recommended lens aperture by $2f$-stops and you will have a good starting point for a successful bounce-flash exposure.

An effective bounce surface should be light-toned and neutral-colored to reflect as much light as possible and to give a natural color appearance. Make sure to aim the flash at a point midway between you and the subject so that the lighting will be even.

CANDID PICTURES

The word candid applies to family holiday cele-brations as well as to stalking an interesting charac-ter on your travels. Your challenge is to photograph people in a natural atmosphere without calling atten-tion to yourself. The reward is capturing the genuine emotions and expressions that give real clues to character.

There are two approaches to candid photography. One is to immerse yourself in whatever is going on, wait until the participants lose interest in you and resume their activity, and then start taking pictures. You can get totally natural, un-self-conscious ex-pressions—real slice-of-life material.

The other way is to find an unobtrusive position where you can remain unnoticed and take your pictures from a distance. Unless you use a camera that accepts auxiliary telephoto lenses, your subjects may appear a bit too distant. A normal or wide-angle lens, such as that found on most snapshot or automatic cameras, helps you get good results when you're in the middle of the action as described at left.

It may be helpful to preset your focus and use a small aperture, a fast shutter speed, and a fast film. This way you can concentrate on your subjects rather than on camera adjustments.

CHILDREN

Children resemble adults in many ways, except that they're smaller and faster. Because they're smaller, you must move closer to get a full-sized image in your picture. You'll also have to get down for an eye-level view. Children behave more naturally when the photographer is on their level.

Because they're so fast, you'll want to take the following precautions. Use a fast shutter speed— 1/250 second or faster, if possible. Use flash indoors to capture the movement. Don't ask for poses or antics until you're completely ready to shoot. Use a high-speed film that will allow you a small aperture for maximum depth of field. (See page 144 for more information about depth of field.) The greater the range in acceptably sharp focus, the better chance you'll have to get sharp pictures of a quick youngster. Needless to say, if you have a game or some activity prearranged in a certain location, you should have all the time you need to take fine pictures while the child is occupied.

Most children have soft, clear skin that doesn't show when harsh shadows are present. Back-lighting, shady spots, and overcast days will portray any child's smooth complexion.

Above
A child's discovery can provide memorable pictures. Make sure to move close. Get down for a better view of the activity and the expressions. Be ready for one or more special moments.

Right
The soft light from a shaded window gently illuminates the subtle tones of a child's skin. Because such a scene is fairly dim, consider a high-speed film for sharp pictures.

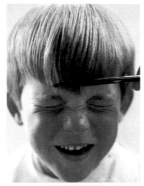

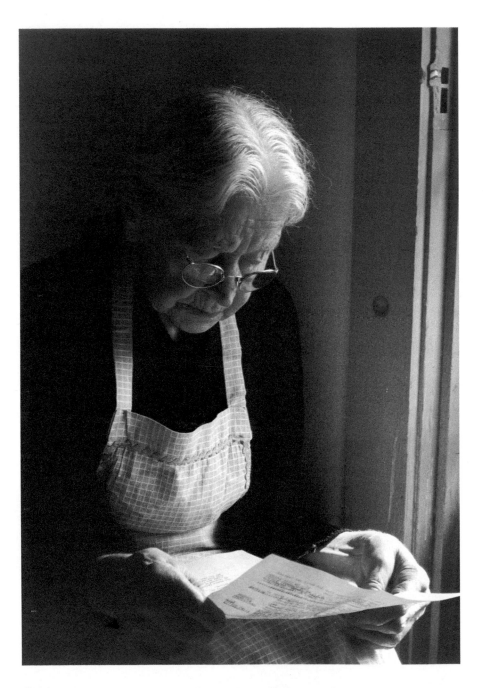

ELDERLY

A flattering portrait calls for soft, even lighting that will play down wrinkles and/or other complexion irregularities. You can make such a portrait outdoors in the shade or on an overcast day or indoors with indirect light from outside. Bounce flash provides another possibility. Your subject will be more relaxed and comfortable if involved in one of his or her typical activities, and you'll get more natural expressions. Remember, keep the picture simple by avoiding or removing objects that will clutter or distract.

On the other hand, if you want to emphasize a character displayed in a weather-beaten face or in gnarled hands, you will want strong directional lighting to give shape to the lines and to enhance the texture. Sidelighting can be very effective for this, and it needn't be terribly harsh. Too strong a light will cause so much contrast that you'll lose the fine gradations between highlight and shadow.

WEDDINGS

The amount of emotion at a wedding is usually far greater than at any other occasion. To the amateur photographer, this is doubly important. First, you'll see more potential pictures than you can probably take. Second, the pictures you do take can have a rich significance in the years to come.

Since everyone wants to have a good time, including the photographer, try to plan ahead. Figure out what activities you want to record and ask the bride for a timetable and a list of locations. Check to see if you can take pictures in the church—particularly if you plan to use flash. If you feel strongly about planning, visit the locations beforehand to choose picture-taking spots and to choose what films you'll want (if there's a possibility of taking existing-light photos).

The next important step is to anticipate activity spots before a crowd gathers. This way you'll have

the best vantage points. Take plenty of pictures. If you think you missed the most dramatic moment of the cake cutting, for instance, persuade the couple to do it again. Incidentally, let the professional photographer cover the wedding without interference. Professionals are fast and decisive and usually will allow you plenty of opportunity to get great shots.

One advantage you'll have is knowing some of the family and guests. Watch the live wires of the crowd for delightful candid snapshots. These informal pictures of people and happenings between the main events will be treasured by all concerned, particularly the bride and groom. In fact, you can give a very nice after-wedding present by making up a small album of your best shots. Everyone remembers weddings through pictures—the more the merrier.

People at weddings are usually paying attention to the proceedings. You get great opportunities to capture friends and relatives being themselves. If you have a loaded camera ready for action, you should get a wonderful collection of memories.

PLACES

Landscapes closely follow people in popularity with most photographers. The reasons are as varied as the pictures, but several stand out—landscapes are beautiful and interesting; they provoke the imagination, and they provide a photographic challenge. Transferring the appearance and emotion of the scene from the mind to the film has been a lifetime quest for some photographers.

How often do photographers revel in the panorama stretched before them only to sigh with disappointment when they view their pictures? Although there are a number of hints that we'll discuss for better scenic shots, the most important advice we can give is: analyze *why* you're struck by a particular view and try to transfer your feelings to camera techniques. Ask these questions:

1. What elements of the scene interest you most? Trees, mountains, water, etc?
2. Do you want mostly sky, land, or water?
3. Is the scene more interesting as a horizontal or as a vertical?
4. Are colors or shapes more important?

Only you can answer these questions, of course, because you are the one who will be looking at the scene. The next few pages will offer some tools to help you get the answers into your pictures.

Pictures are reminders. As time passes, the memories get dimmer and dimmer. Moods and feelings are particularly difficult to recapture. Pictures help keep those memories bright—memories of the places you've seen and the wonders that leave you breathless. It's important to consider some of the ways to capture the sensations you feel in a particular place. Lighting and camera position are especially important. Notice in the picture at right how the slanting shadows of early morning help to define the shapes and bulk of the seaside cliffs. See also the subtle impression of distance offered by the haze in the scene. These ideas and others will be discussed in this chapter.

Question 1. Whatever part of the scene interests you the most, concentrate on it. No matter how vast the sight, you need one important center of interest. Otherwise the picture will lack impact. Making your camera respond usually means moving closer (making the subject bigger) and possibly shifting angles to eliminate anything extra and unwanted.

Question 2. If the sky is an important element in the picture, aim the camera up to capture more sky, less land. If the sky only provides a horizon, aim the camera down for less sky.

Question 3. If the scene is broad and magnificent, such as a mountain-range horizon, hold the camera horizontally. If the scene seems to stretch from your toes into the distance—a river or a highway—for instance—then hold the camera vertically.

Horizontal

Vertical

Question 4. Sometimes dark shapes and light shapes interact in a way that catches your eye. Find a position and aim your camera so that you concentrate on those shapes only. Anything else in the picture only serves to dilute the image. At other times, you'll see colors interplay in a provocative way. Again, choose a location and aim your camera so that the areas of color dominate the picture.

Dark and light shapes

COMPOSITION

Good composition means placing the elements of a picture in a harmonious, interesting, and even unusual way to capture attention. In setting up a composition, consider the following:

Rule of thirds

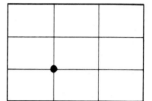

Balance. Do you want a symmetrical arrangement or a casual collection? A symmetrical design has obvious balance. But even an informal composition is balanced so that it feels complete and stable. Colors, shadows, and light areas tend to balance each other and are affected by big shapes, little shapes, distance, and lines.

Rule of Thirds. A traditional way that artists have grouped elements in pictures is called the rule of thirds. Place the center of interest and important subordinate elements near intersections of vertical and horizontal lines at 1/3 points of the picture.

Framing

Scale

Perspective. How do you make a two-dimensional picture express the depth and vastness of a three-dimensional scene? Carefully. Here are ideas.

Framing means almost surrounding your distant subject with some nearby foreground material, such as overhanging branches. The contrast between the near objects and the distant subject can help to establish distance. Framing is also helpful for disguising a dull, boring sky or hiding unwanted scene elements.

Similar to framing is the general use of objects in the foreground as subjects for scale to measure the background. Almost anything can be effective: a car, cactus, boulder, relative, motorcycle, boat (on water, of course), cabin, and more. The size of your scale subject will help give an impression of distance. If too close, viewers will forget the scene. At a medium distance, the comparison may be most striking; at a greater distance, the reference presents a more subtle view, but the viewer who stops for a second glance may be awed by how the landscape swallows up the extra subject.

79

Planes

Lines

Planes. Some stunning views, particularly from high up in the mountains and desert, show subjects at different distances. Parallel mountain ranges (running across your field of vision) become hazy as they become more distant. This phenomenon is called aerial perspective. It is particularly obvious in the photo above, taken in Brazil at an early-morning hour when mist still shrouded the cone-like peaks. In the desert, beige sands turn foggy blue near the horizon. Use these separate planes of different color to help establish distance and scale.

Lines. Lines that lead far into the scene can also help establish distance. A fence, a row of telephone poles, a road, or a river, all shrink as they recede from the camera, and this will be captured on film. Lines can also help to draw near and distant areas together into a harmonious picture. The cultivated rows in the picture at the left provide continuous threads that link foreground and background into a single, tranquil scene.

Frontlighting

Backlighting

LIGHTING

Lighting Angles. If you recall the discussion of lighting angles in the "People" section (page 50), you'll remember frontlighting, sidelighting, and backlighting. Although generalizing is always dangerous, sidelighting may be the most effective landscape lighting. Perhaps it's wise to broaden sidelighting to include any angle that does not produce direct frontlighting or backlighting.

You need shadows to help show distance. Frontlighting gives no shadows. Backlighting can give dramatic shadows, but your subject may become a silhouette. Sidelighting from a wide series of angles casts shadows that help you gain an illusion of perspective. Waiting for the right times of day or carefully choosing your position may be the best answers.

Sidelighting

Time and Light. As you've noticed, the landscape changes appearance dramatically from dawn to dusk and throughout the seasons. Obviously, seasonal changes mean green leaves, red leaves, or no leaves, as well as snow or soft grass. But the subtle changes come with changes in the light. Winter light is harsh but weak; summer light is rich but often oppressive. Sunlight in fall and spring is bright and cheerful. At noon, the sun's rays beat straight down, flattening form and perspective. Early in the morning and late afternoon the light is a rich, warm color and long shadows streak across the scene.

Although you can't always choose the season, especially when traveling, you can often select the best time of day to make your landscape photographs. Early morning may be misty with light of a delicate rose color. Shadows are soft and violet, and the distance may be smoky. At noon, the smaller shadows are hard and dense. Distance may be difficult to show. In the late afternoon, the light becomes more orange and the large shadows are warm and rich. The distance may be clear but will contrast in blue against the warmer foreground.

TRAVEL

Many people take most of their year's pictures during vacation or travel times. They see new sights and enjoy exciting experiences—experiences they want to deposit in their memory banks and share with others.

Travel photography combines all the elements discussed in this book—people, landscapes, interesting objects, flowers, night scenes, and sports. The challenge is being ready for all at the same time. Here are some general ideas, followed by specific tips, that should make your travel photography easier.

Research. As you plan the details of your trip, list important sights that you'll want to photograph. Then you'll have a ready reference to assist your memory. Of course, you'll find special places of interest not listed in any guide book. Many of these will give your pictures a more authentic local flavor than the customary landmarks—the early-morning marketplace, people involved in unique craft work, unusual methods of transportation, and, of course, the preparation of those special meals.

Early-morning shadows and foreground branches create perspective in this gorgeous view of Neuschwanstein Castle near Fussen, Germany.

*Right
Pictures of people add character to your travel memories. Ask permission and get a winning expression from a classical dancer in Cochin, India.*

Take Plenty of Pictures. Once back home, the typical sentiment is, "Why didn't we take more?" Film is a small part of your travel budget, but the pictures will be a large part of later enjoyment.

Look for the best angles and positions from which to photograph your subjects. Sometimes you'll find that you can improve the composition of your first picture by shifting your position.

When photographing colorful, fast-moving events, keep looking through the viewfinder. Take pictures as often as you see something you like.

Many Subjects. Be prepared to move in close, with permission of course, to people in native or ethnic dress. Photograph camel caravans, shop windows full of curios, floral displays, festivals, parades, local sports, children, building interiors, and illuminated sights at night. Remember that many of your best-treated pictures will be of the subjects you found unique—the ones that you reacted to most strongly. Also, don't worry about bad weather. Fine photos can come from inclement conditions—umbrellas in the rain, fishing boats at anchor in the fog, and children playing in the snow.

Be Prepared. Keep your camera with you at all times, ready and loaded, and be alert for good picture situations.

Tell a Story. Your travel pictures should describe the vacation as completely as possible. Don't forget to capture events that will help you remember. Airplane flights, train trips, taxi rides, customs officials, hotels, tour guides—all these contribute to the later enjoyment of your vacation. Many travelers photograph signs as memory joggers. Signs are even better when familiar faces surround them.

Personalize Your Pictures. Have family or tour-group members pose in pictures of monuments, scenic views, restaurants, and with the helpful local people you'll meet. You'll delight in the warmer significance of these scenes later.

Tips. Here are some specifics that might help.

1. Before you leave home, look at your list of possible pictures, and pack about twice as much film as you think you'll need.

2. Allow enough time to expose a roll of film and have it processed before you leave. It's a good way to make sure that your camera is operating correctly.

3. During travel preparation, register all foreign-made photo equipment with U.S. customs, so that misunderstandings about duty won't arise on your return. Most Federal office buildings include a Custom House office where an official will inventory your equipment and give you the proper document to surrender to customs officials when you return. Sales receipts may be enough documentation.

4. Don't forget flash pictures. Take whatever batteries, flash devices, or current transformers you'll need.

5. When passing through airport security, ask for hand-inspection of your camera and all film, exposed and unexposed. It's not always possible. Security x-rays can be harmful to your film—the more x-rays the worse the harm. Anytime you avoid the x-ray scanners will help the final results. When using a higher-speed film, such as KODAKCOLOR GOLD 1600 Film, it is especially important to protect it from x-rays.

6. It is a sensible practice to examine your camera at night after touring is finished for the day. Clean the lens, if necessary, and check the battery if your camera uses one. Make sure that the carrying strap is secure.

7. Keep your camera with you—to avoid theft and to keep ready for picture-taking opportunities. An unattended camera can be an inviting prize.

PETS

Pets have as much personality as people, and pictures should communicate those traits. You'll need some ingenuity, lots of patience, and a good location. Small animals, of course, can be photographed nearly anywhere. Larger pets will give you less choice. Above all, find a setting that appears natural.

Animals, like children, have limited patience and a short attention span. Set up your camera and get

Horses might be best in a field.

A working dog might be best in a field, a house cat on a window sill or in front of the fire. Try to keep the background simple.

Flash is an effective way to separate a small animal from confusing surroundings indoors. Flash can also stop quick movement. Move in close enough to eliminate other elements in the picture.

Make sure that you stay in the minimum focus range of the camera. Also, see that you are still within the flash range of your camera. If you are still in focus, but too close for the flash, put one or two layers of white tissue over the flash to cut down the light. When you're all set to take a flash picture, try to spark an interesting expression.

completely ready to take pictures before you bring your subject on stage.

Ingenuity means keeping your pet in the same place and evoking appealing, enthusiastic expressions. Find or devise a noisemaker that will perk up your pet's ears for an alert look. Getting a pet to stay may call for a morsel of favorite food.

Be patient. When you see what you want, take plenty of pictures. Pets soon grow restless.

Get fairly close—enough so that your subject fills the viewfinder. Place the camera down at the pet's eye level, just as you would for a small child. The perspective gives a less distorted view, and animals appreciate the eye-level approach.

Some animals have special photogenic habits. Famous animal photographer Walter Chandoha made one of his first commercially successful pet photos of his cat Minguina, who made a long stretch in front of a mirror after every nap. Chandoha got ready and snapped her in the middle of the stretch—just what an eager art director wanted for an advertisement.

Most pets can move pretty fast when inspired. Practice the stunt you want to capture with an unloaded camera. When everything looks right, start taking pictures.

ZOOS

Everybody likes the zoo, and your zoo photos should show it. You can take pictures of the animals and pictures of people enjoying the animals. For best results in photographing the animals themselves, get as close as safely possible. Dangerous inhabitants are usually behind bars, wire, or glass. From behind the barriers in a safe position, aim your camera through the wire or between the bars or put it right next to the glass. Make sure to stay behind zoo-imposed barriers. Wild animals are always unpredictable. There's no sense offering yourself as a free meal if the city has already provided one.

Where there are fewer restrictions, it's easier to get unobstructed photos. As always, see if you can find a position with superior lighting and background. Move around until you find the best setting.

The petting zoo is often one of the most fertile areas for great, spontaneous pictures—especially with your kids. Most youngsters are thrilled and awed by all the furry, friendly creatures, and their faces show it. Move in close enough to capture those rapturous expressions.

Some zoos have indoor displays where you can take flash pictures (pages 152-161) or existing-light pictures (see page 165) of the exhibits. Put camera and flash next to the glass where possible. Where you're separated from the glass, take your pictures at an angle so that flash reflections won't bounce back at your camera.

You can get fantastic results at the attractions where spectators are caged in autos and the inhabitants roam free. The wild animals are familiar with autos and will venture quite close. Use extreme caution, however, and carefully obey the rules. A charging carnivore has more primitive things in mind than portrait photography. If you're in a car with the windows down, just stay inside the window. If the windows are closed and the car is moving, hold the camera next to but not touching the glass. You'll avoid reflections and get sharper pictures. Use as fast shutter speed as possible to overcome car or animal movement.

Surprisingly, time of day may be important for zoo pictures. At peak visitation periods during the weekend, the animals may retire to their hideaways just to avoid the crowds. Midday is usually a time for napping in the animal kingdom. Try to schedule a special trip with friends or family to see the creatures when they're likely to be most active— during the week, preferably in the morning before feeding time.

FLOWERS AND PLANTS

Any flower garden is a cornucopia of nature's greatest treasures—dazzling colors and soft fragrances combined in a master patchwork of cosmic design. Some "gardens" are wild, growing free, while others are carefully planned and cultivated. In either case, there are some simple techniques that should give you exciting pictures.

Concentrate on the garden—move in close enough to picture only the blooms. Better yet, take pictures at different distances to show the overall view and then smaller segments of floral glory. Get very close with close-up lenses. (See page 182.) Move around so that you have the best background and picture design. Take pictures when the light makes nature's work most attractive. The best times are early in the morning with soft shadows and sparkling dew or the rich, warm light of late afternoon.

Take pictures throughout the growing season so that you have a complete record to share with distant friends or relatives.

Look for exciting pictures of nature subjects in all the seasons. Fall leaves, snow-covered pine needles, and the first crocuses give extra dimension to the year's picture-taking.

Close-Up Tips. A piece of colored construction paper will provide a simple background that concentrates attention on your subject. Electronic flash or a piece of white cardboard will reflect light into shadow areas. Since you'll be very close, cover a flash with two or more layers of tissue for correct exposure. If the breeze is batting your subject around, make a quick windbreak of tomato stakes and sheet plastic. For that extra-fresh look, create some artificial dew with an atomizer.

BUILDINGS

What's important about a particular building? Or, rather, why do you like a special building? What are the features that attract you? Once you've isolated these aspects, concentrate on them.

In the photograph above, the photographer sensed peace and stability in the weatherbeaten harbor structures. This feeling is augmented by the nearly perfect reflection. Although cropped for best page

design, the breadth of the long, low buildings is captured by horizontal framing. The misty surroundings
create a mood of New England nostalgia which
seems to await the arrival of a transatlantic square-
rigger. Another case might show a martial line of
brilliantly gingerbreaded row houses. Naturally,
you'll want to capture the pattern of the group, as
well as individual details.

Details might be ornate or stately entrances, wrought-iron work, or designs in the brick or stonework of the facade. Again, wait for a time of day when the light shows off your subject, and move in close to isolate what you want to capture.

Collectibles and Objets D'Art. Many hobbyists make or collect things that they want to show other like-minded people. They also see things on display that they want to record. Same important rules—move in close (with a close-up lens, if necessary. See page 182). Find a camera position that sees a simple background, and use lighting that shows off the object's best features. If necessary, use reflectors to fill in shadows. One good way to control your results is to cover a table with plain cloth or paper, preferably not white, that contrasts with your subject. Raise the cloth or paper up out of focus in the background to provide an undistracting backdrop. Outdoors in sunlight, you can control the lighting by turning the table. Indoors with photolamps (see page 58), you can move the lights.

The free-form ceramic statuettes pictured at left were photographed in the set-up shown above. Indirect window light provided the main illumination, while a white reflector card filled the dark-side shadows.

ACTION

There are some familiar ideas for capturing action successfully as well as several specific techniques. Following a few general tips are ideas about portraying movement.

Get as close as you safely can. Choose a position that will dramatize the action. Look for an uncluttered background and good lighting. Preset your camera controls and focus on the spot where you plan to capture your subject. When the moving body arrives at the spot, snap the picture. When composing the picture, leave a little room in front of your subject—it looks more natural.

STOPPING THE ACTION

You can usually freeze movement sharply in one of four ways. You can set a fast shutter speed on your camera (see pages 138-141). The faster the shutter speed, the more likely your chances of capturing a sharp-moving subject. Camera position will help, too. You can also catch some movement at its peak, or you can pan your camera with the subject.

Peak of Action. Some motions have a midpoint where everything stops momentarily. A diver at the top of an upward spring or a basketball player up for a dunk both stop before descending. A baseball pitcher or hitter, a tennis player, and a golfer all pause before moving and stop after their follow-through. Practice for a while without film. Follow a diver to the mid-air pause and pretend you're snapping that fraction of a second. Get a golfing friend to practice swings. See if you can capture the stationary highpoint of both backswing and follow-through.

Panning. Panning works with running kids, dogs, horses, bicycles, race cars, speed boats, or airplanes during take off. You may have to pan for two reasons. First, the subject may be moving so fast that even a fast shutter speed cannot stop the action. Second, good composition is difficult because the subject is in your viewfinder for such a short time. Swing both your camera and body so that the moving subject stays in the same place in your viewfinder. This, too, takes practice. Rotate your body smoothly and concentrate on pressing the shutter-release button at the best point for picture design. Follow through after you snap the shutter. Unless you can choose a very fast shutter speed, chances are good that the subject will be sharp and the background will be blurred into attractive streaks of color.

Toward the camera

Direction. The direction of movement may affect your choice of technique. A subject coming toward or retreating from you is easier to capture sharply than one crossing your field of vision. You can use a slower shutter speed for action toward or away from you, and you'll find that you have more time to make a good composition. Subjects moving at a 90° angle to you and your camera invite panning and your fastest shutter speeds.

1/500 second at 90 °

1/30 second at 90 °

BLURRED ACTION

Blurred motion can convey the idea of speed and movement. Set a very slow shutter speed (1/30 to 1/8 second) on your camera. You can pan or hold the camera steady while the subject's blurred movements cover a little bigger slice of time on your film. When the camera is mounted on a tripod or other solid support, only the subject will be blurred. Add your own movement by handholding the camera.

SPORTS TIPS

Get close to the players. Ask permission for a sideline spot at amateur and school competitions. At professional events choose an unobstructed position as near the action as possible.

Prefocus on the spot where you'll get the best picture. Have your camera loaded and the exposure controls set. It's very helpful to know the game, because you can anticipate key plays and key players. Photograph night games and indoor events by the existing light. See pages 162-165.

NIGHT

The world spends half its time in light and half in darkness. Picture-taking at night can be just as exciting as daytime photography.

You'll find subjects everywhere—bright lights, fireworks, holiday displays, and outdoor activities. Snapshot camera owners can use flash outdoors at night. A high-speed film will extend the flash range. Owners of automatic or adjustable cameras can take pictures with flash or with the existing light. High-speed films, slow shutter speeds, and a large maximum aperture will help capture almost anything that you can see. See pages 162-165 for more existing-light recommendations.

BAD WEATHER

Everybody takes pictures when the sun is out. But on some days, it rains, snows, mists, or is just plain overcast. The truth is that some of your best pictures can happen on days with poor weather. Think of the benefits.

People look their best out of the sun. Their faces open up with bright, natural, unshadowed expressions. Light overcast days are perfect for outstanding portraits. Just make sure that your background doesn't include much dull sky and move in close to your subject. You may even find that rain and snow give people, kids especially, an opportunity to wear colorful clothing and engage in activities you'll want to capture. In rain or snow, take care to protect your camera. Keep it warm and dry under a raincoat or in your camera bag. These precautionary measures, however, don't necessarily apply to all-weather cameras (see page 21).

Scenery takes on a very different appearance on a dull day. Although the sky appears gloomy and grim, the colors of grass and trees, red barns, and white fences can appear brighter. Fog will lend an ethereal quality to many scenes—subjects may appear partly shrouded in mist. Subjects may appear bluish in pictures made while the sun is hiding. Attach an 81A filter* to your camera lens to warm up the colors a bit. You won't need to change your exposure.

Snow and cold give a soft, blurred appearance in pastel shades. With your camera protected from snowflakes and the cold, you'll find a world full of children, sleds, snowmen, skiers, and colorful outerwear. At night, you can take unusual flash pictures of nearby subjects with snowflakes hovering all around.

Rain brings some charming surprises—bright umbrellas and colorful rain gear, for instance. Reflections in puddles or on rain-drenched streets give another dimension to your pictures. Keep your camera out of the water, but don't hesitate to shoot activity in a rainshower. Find a good position to snap the action from under an overhang, or inside a car with the window open.

*See pages 170-171 for more on filters.

Overcast skies give delightful, casual portraits, because your subjects won't be squinting into the sun. Try not to include much of the dull sky, and you'll find bright, colorful subjects all around. Again, high-speed film will help you get well-exposed pictures with a snapshot camera. Remember that your family and other people don't suspend activity when the sun goes under. Sometimes a gloomy day will inspire children to try something new. If they don't think of anything, suggest an interesting activity that will get them occupied and yield good pictures.

Mist or fog can lend a ghostly, ethereal appearance to familiar scenes. Nearby subjects will be distinct, but more distant subjects will seem to be fading into another dimension. Often, there's bright light com-

ing through the mist, spotlighting bright objects or making trails through the heavy air. Early morning is a perfect time to search out misty scenes. If the sky is dark overhead, use a high-speed film in a snapshot camera.

EXPOSURE
Bad weather is darker, and you'll need more exposure than in sunlight. See pages 132-141 for film choice and exposure-setting information. Automatic cameras, of course, will adjust to scene lighting with very little help from you. Use high-speed film in a snapshot camera.

SHOWING YOUR PICTURES

Good pictures are meant to be seen. Here are some ideas for getting more mileage from your best efforts. (Make sure you read page 115 for information about storing and protecting your photos.)

PHOTO ALBUMS

Albums abound in shapes and sizes from purse-size books to coffee-table volumes. You can also make your own with a loose-leaf binder, thin cardboard pages, and photo cement. Many people assemble their albums chronologically—it seems sensible. They also label the pictures *and* the negative-envelopes so that they can order reprints easily at a later date.

Some people get more in albums by cutting up the prints and inserting the best parts. There's wasted space in almost every print.

A photo album can be the chronicle of years or an up-to-date newsbrief filled with your latest snapshots.

ENLARGEMENTS AND HOME DECOR

Another way to get your best images out of the box and into view is to display enlargements. They are available from your photofinisher in different sizes from 5 x 7 inches to poster-print size and in shapes to fit your film format. Enlargements are ideal for framing or for gifts. Hung on a wall, displayed on a desk, or even commanding an important place in your albums, enlargements have a powerful ability to cross the barriers of time and say, "You were there." For more ideas on decorating with photographs, see the KODAK Publication *Photo Decor,* available from your photo dealer.

Traditional and unusual ways of displaying prints are available from your local photo, stationery, department, or discount store. You'll see frames in dozens of styles as well as such different ideas as photo cubes, wall clocks, mobiles, and collage boards.

GREETING CARDS

A card with a picture of you or you and your family is a truly personal communication. Children grow, houses change, and so do the seasons. You can commission special greetings from your photofinishers with pictures and words printed together, or you can attach a print to the inside of other cards. Some people plan ahead and have favorite shots reprinted to enclose in letters to distant friends and relatives. A photo holiday card each year keeps the people on your mailing list in closer touch with a growing family.

PROCESSING SERVICES

In addition to reprints, enlargements, and photo-greeting cards, your photofinisher can make slides from negatives, prints and enlargements from slides, and copyprints from other prints. Some photofinishers can help you crop the negatives you want enlarged to improve the picture composition.

Greeting cards for many occasions are available from your photofinisher. Can you guess which holiday cards receive the most attention?

STORING PICTURES

With a little care and forethought, your pictures will provide many years of pleasure. Here are some ideas for prolonging the lives of prints, slides, and negatives.

Choose a place with moderate temperature (under 70°F [21°C]) and fairly low humidity (under 50% relative humidity). This probably eliminates most basements and attics. Heat can become excessive in an attic, and humidity in either place may be harmful. A spot near a chimney, heat run, or in direct window light can also cause problems.

An album is the best way to display and protect your prints. However, make sure that the materials used in the album will not harm the prints. Check with your photo dealer about the cover, pages, plastic sleeves, mounting corners or hinges, cement, and the ink used for identification. This is especially important if you don't have the negatives for reprinting.

Don't subject prints to pressure by stacking or crowding albums tightly on a shelf. Don't let the image sides of the prints contact each other directly; protect them in an album with a suitable plastic sheeting.

Make sure that the adhesive you use to mount the prints is photographically safe. Don't use starch paste, animal glue, or rubber cement. One of the safest methods is using special dry-mounting tissue. Ask your photo dealer for specific recommendations.

Find a safe home for negatives and extra prints. Most photofinishers provide envelopes that are safe for storing prints and negatives; they contain no contaminants that would ruin the images. Other containers may have ingredients that will quickly harm photos. Furniture drawers, attics, and basements where fumes from mothballs, cosmetics, chemicals, glues, or wood-finishing products can also cause damaging chemical reactions.

Don't store prints and negatives under pressure— they may stick together. If you have real favorites, separate them into plastic photo sleeves for safekeeping.

SLIDE SHOWS

Most people who use slides like to see that big, bright image up on the screen. Because it's so big, it can be shared with many people at the same time, and modern projection equipment can show many slides in a comparatively short time. On the other hand, everyone nods in sympathy when a friend mentions that three of last evening's hours were devoted to someone's slide show or home movies. With a little planning and restraint, you can have your audiences clamoring for more.

First, arrange your slides so that they tell a story, even if it's a simple chronological story of vacation travel. You'll find that narration is easier when you can proceed logically from one topic to the next. Second, use only your best slides. Pass over pictures that are fuzzy or incorrectly exposed. Resist the temptation to show everything. Third, don't leave any one slide on the screen too long—10 seconds is a

Selecting pictures

Choose only your best pictures—ones that are sharp and correctly exposed. Poor-quality pictures are tiring to view and lower the impact of your show. One easy way to look at slides is with the help of an inexpensive illuminator, available from most photo dealers. Project your final choices to check their sharpness.

useful, average time. If you have to spend a long time explaining a picture, chances are that it's not a very good illustration. Your audience is used to TV and movies where things generally happen pretty fast. Fourth, consider one hour the maximum time that people can sit still comfortably. Fifth, rehearse your presentation a few times, so that you're familiar with the order of the slides and so that your narration will flow easily. Sixth, get everything—screen, projector, and chairs—set up in advance. And make sure that you have a spare projector bulb and know how to change it.

Telling a Story
The easiest way to tell a story with pictures is to put them in chronological order. Since every story has certain key elements or events, use the pictures that best portray the highpoints. You don't have to explain or show every step. Just include the necessary pictures. Too many will dilute the message.

1. Getting ready

2. Frosting the cake

3. Making the presentation

PHOTO REPORTS

There are times when photos are more striking than words alone. Reports for business, school, and even your community are more effective when amplified by pictures. You can create a slide show or illustrate a written report with captioned prints, or consider enlargement displays in public places. Here's what's important. The pictures should clearly show exactly what you want them to show. Use no more than you need—too many dilute impact. Make sure that the technical quality is good—sharp and well-exposed pictures. Captions or narration should be short and to the point.

PHOTO INVENTORY

Nobody likes to face the idea of calamity, but that's why insurance companies exist. In case of a loss, it's helpful to provide as much evidence as possible. Pictures can be valuable resources.

Take a moment to make a mental inventory of your possessions and how much it would cost to replace them. With this incentive, you might want to load and use your camera. A series of photographs can effectively document your goods, particularly when combined with the sales receipts.

Start with your home—the outside and the inside. Take pictures outside when the scene is bright and when important features aren't hidden in shadow. Shoot from all important viewpoints and maybe a few more for extra precaution. When inside, take pictures of the four walls in each room with flash or existing light. (Don't forget to include some of the floor with costly rugs or carpet.)

Once you have covered all the exterior and interior features of the house, begin recording from a closer distance the smaller items such as silver flatware, fine china, paintings, objets d'art, clothes, tools, small appliances, sports equipment, antique furniture, and jewelry. The same applies to lawn and garden equipment, outside furniture, and so on.

Keep the prints and negatives or slides in your safe deposit box in case you ever need them to prove a loss.

HAS IT HAPPENED TO YOU?

Sometimes things go wrong and you get results you didn't plan *or* want. Here are some of the most common problems, the reasons, and some suggested solutions.

Camera movement

Out of focus

Problem	Reason	Solution
Fuzzy, unsharp pictures.	Shutter speed too slow.	For pictures of still subjects, use a shutter speed no slower than 1/30 second if handholding the camera. For fast-moving subjects, use the fastest shutter speed possible—usually no slower than 1/250 second. (See page 141.)
	Incorrect handling.	Make sure you hold the camera very steady and gently press the shutter-release button. (See pages 42-44.)
	Incorrect focus.	Make sure you focus correctly on your subject. Refer to your camera manual. (See page 43.)
	Dirty lens.	Keep your lens clean of dust and smears. (See page 186.)

Dirty lens

Problem	Reason	Solution
Pictures too light, too dark.	Incorrect film-speed setting on camera or on handheld meter.	Set or check the film speed every time you load a new roll of film.
	Dead or weak meter battery.	Check battery periodically according to camera manual. Replace at least once a year.
	No adjustment for side- and back-lighting.	See page 142 for information about adjusting for different lighting angles.
Pictures occasionally too light.	Shutter may be sticking.	See competent camera repair person.
Blank negatives (no prints) or black slides.	Shutter did not open.	See camera repair person.
	Film did not advance through camera.	Check loading procedures in manual or have repair person check film-advance mechanism.
	Lens cap not removed.	Make sure you remove lens cap.
Pictures consistently too light or dark.	Exposure meter may need adjustment.	See repair person.

Too light

Correct exposure

Too dark

Problem	Reason	Solution
Flash pictures too light, dark.	Light—too close to subject. Dark—too far from subject.	Check snapshot-camera distance-range or check focus setting with adjustable/ automatic camera. (See page 153.)
	Film speed on camera/flash unit wrong.	Check to see that correct film speed is set on flash unit or camera. (See page 154.)
	Aperture setting wrong.	Make sure that aperture setting on camera agrees with information on flash calculator dial. (See pages 155-156.)
Flash too dark.	Dark—electronic flash may not have fully recycled.	Allow flash to recycle fully until ready light shows or maybe a bit longer.
	Weak batteries.	(See page 157.) Change batteries.
People or animals with glowing eyes.	Flash positioned too close to lens for subject with open retina.	Turn on all room lights. If possible, remove flash from camera to increase distance between lens and flash. Increase flash-to-subject distance. Have person avert eyes.

Too dark

Correctly exposed

Too light

Problem	Reason	Solution
Flash pictures: black slides, blank negatives, and no prints.	Flash didn't fire.	Battery dead, poor connection between flash and camera. (See page 154.)
Glare spots in flash pictures.	Flash aimed into reflective background.	Adjust your position so that any reflective material (mirrors, paneled walls, eyeglasses) is at an angle.
Flash pictures unevenly exposed.	Foreground object closer than main subject—gets overexposed.	Use a position where the main subject is closest to the flash.
Flash pictures partly exposed.	Incorrect shutter speed.	Check your camera manual for correct shutter speed with flash. (See page 154.)

Foreground object

Object removed

Wrong shutter speed

Reflection from shiny surface

Position changed to avoid reflection

123

Problem	Reason	Solution
Pictures with dark obstructions.	Finger in front of lens. Material inside camera.	Check camera-holding position to make sure hand or fingers don't obstruct lens. Carefully check inside camera for foreign matter obstruction.
	Camera strap or case in front of lens.	Check that lens is clear of strap and case before taking picture.
Pictures with unusual color.	Bluish—tungsten film used in daylight.	Make sure that the film matches the lighting conditions. If not, add a filter. (See page 168.)
	Yellowish-red—daylight film used in tungsten light.	If using daylight film in tungsten light, consider a filter. (See page 168.)
	Mottled, streaked, maybe greenish or muddy—film outdated.	Make sure you use fresh film and have it processed promptly. Check packing material for expiration date. Do not leave film in extremely hot places.

Finger blocking lens

Tungsten film in daylight

Daylight film in tungsten light

Problem	Reason	Solution
Pictures overlapped.	Too many pictures on roll.	Don't try to squeeze one more shot at the end of the roll.
	Film winding mechanism needs adjustment.	See a competent repair person.
Light streaks and spots on pictures.	Direct rays of light strike lens.	Don't shoot directly into the sun or other bright light source.
Consistent streaks and spots.	Fogging: light leak in camera.	Have camera checked by competent repair person.
	Camera back opened accidentally.	Never open the camera without checking to see if it has film inside.
	Film handled in direct sunlight.	Load and unload your camera in the shade or other subdued light.
	Sticking shutter.	Have camera checked by competent repair person.
	X-ray exposure.	Ask for hand inspection of camera and film by airport security. (See page 89.)

Overlapped pictures

Direct rays of light

Camera back opened

SIMPLIFYING THE TECHNICALITIES

The more you know about any skill or activity, the better the results. This section of *How to Take Good Pictures* is devoted to how photography works and how to extend your knowledge for even better pictures under a greater variety of conditions.

We'll approach our goal—good pictures—in two ways. First we'll take a tour of a simple 35 mm camera to see what functions all the controls perform. We'll look at film to see what makes it work for you. We'll tie film camera together into a discussion of exposure that will help you get better results in many tricky situations.

Then, after discussing the sketchy fundamentals of how you can control camera and film, we'll talk about some individual techniques that you'll want to sample. Flash, filters, existing light, and more will show you the delight of creation, where *you* control *your* photography.

CAMERA CONTROLS

All cameras have controls. The simplest camera might have only one control—the shutter-release button which you press to take a picture.

More complicated cameras may have several controls. Earlier in the book, we gave a short discussion of 35 mm camera operation—enough to help you start. Now we'll take an imaginary automatic 35 mm camera and describe the function of all the moving parts you need to know about. Your camera may have some or all the features we'll describe. And very likely some of the devices will be in different positions from those shown here. Compare these diagrams to those in your camera manual.

For greater clarity, we've even repeated some functions. For example, if your camera has a pop-up flash, you probably won't have a flash hot shoe or a flash-cord socket.

Top Front View

1. *film-advance lever*
2. *film-frame counter*
3. *shutter-release button*
4. *shutter-speed dial*
5. *flash hot shoe*
6. *rewind knob*
7. *pop-up flash*
8. *pop-up flash button*
9. *viewfinder window*
10. *lens*
11. *aperture ring and mode selector (automatic, manual, possibly flash)*
12. *focusing ring*
13. *film-speed selector dial*
14. *self-timer*
15. *flash-cord socket*

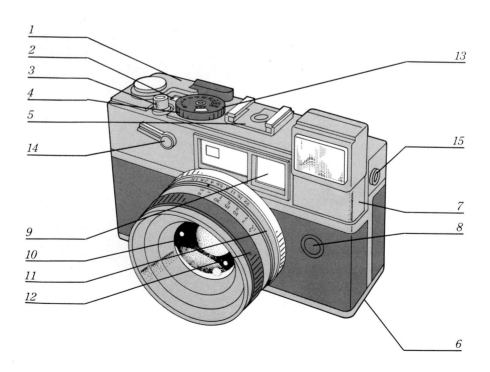

1. Film-advance lever. *By moving this lever one or more strokes after taking a picture, you advance the film to the next frame.*

2. Film-frame counter. *This shows you how many pictures you have taken: from loading steps to 12, 20, 24, or 36.*

3. Shutter-release button. *You press this button to take a picture.*

4. Shutter-speed dial. *This selects the shutter speed. It may include the film-speed selector or the automatic-operation switch.*

5. Flash hot shoe. *This accepts an electronic flash unit. When you attach the flash, the electrical connection is complete.*

6. Rewind knob. *This knob usually has a foldout lever to help rewind exposed film back into the magazine.*

7. Pop-up flash. *Raise and activate built-in flash with the button shown in callout 8. Turn off the flash by pressing down.*

8. Pop-up flash button. *This button raises and activates the built-in flash unit.*

9. Viewfinder window. *This is the other side of the window you look through to compose your picture.*

10. **Lens.** *The lens on your camera gathers and organizes light rays to make a sharp picture on your film.*

11. **Aperture ring.** *With this you select the lens aperture. The aperture ring may also control automatic, manual, or flash functions.*

12. **Focusing ring.** *You turn this to get sharp pictures of your subject. It may show distances as symbols or in feet and metres.*

Back View

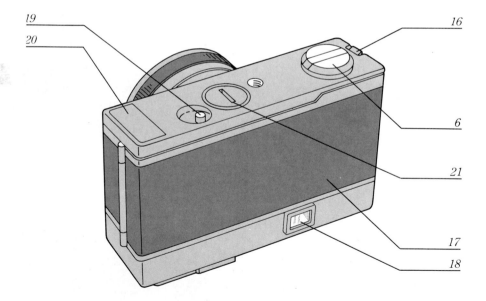

16. release for film-
    compartment door
17. film-compartment door

18. viewfinder window
19. film-advance release
    button

20. pop-up flash battery
    compartment
21. meter-battery
    compartment

13. Film-speed selector dial. *Every time you load film into your camera, set the film speed on the selector dial.*

14. Self-timer. *This device automatically snaps the shutter after it is triggered, which allows you to include yourself in the picture.*

15. Flash-cord socket. *Plug the flash cord (PC cord) into this socket to complete the electronic connection between the flash and the camera.*

16. Release for film-compartment door. *After you rewind the exposed film, open the compartment door with this latch.*

17. Film-compartment door. *By operating the latch in callout 16, this door can be opened to load or unloaded film.*

18. Viewfinder window. *You look through this window to arrange your picture. You may also see focusing and exposure information.*

19. Film-advance release button. *This button releases the film-advance mechanism so that you can rewind the film.*

20. Pop-up flash battery compartment. *This compartment holds the batteries that supply the power to your built-in electronic flash.*

21. Meter-battery. *The battery for automatic or manual cameras with exposure meters should be changed at least once a year.*

FILM

Black-and-white negative   *Color negative*   *Color slide*

In addition to the film information on page 48, the following information will help you understand the next section on exposure.

SIZE

Film comes in different sizes and lengths: 110 for pocket-sized cameras, 126 for larger snapshot cameras, and 135 for 35 mm cameras. Films in 110 and 126 sizes generally give a choice of 12 or 24 exposures for color prints, 20 exposures for color slides. Film in 135-size magazines offers 12, 24, and 36 exposures.

SLIDES OR PRINTS

Do you want slides to project or prints from negatives to pass around and put in albums? Slides projected on a screen are brilliant and beautiful, but slide film requires near-perfect exposure for good results. Prints are lovely, too, and are convenient to share. Negative film is also more tolerant of exposure error. You can have enlargements made from either slides or negatives.

Bright —low- or medium-speed film

Dim —high- or very high-speed film

SPEED

All films have measured sensitivity to light, indicated by an ISO number. Low- and medium-speed films— ISO 25, 64, 125, 200—are intended for general picture-taking in daylight, while high- and very high-speed films with ISO 400, 1000, and 1600, are intended for low light. If you take pictures on dark days, indoors, or at night without flash, you'll want a high- or very high-speed film.

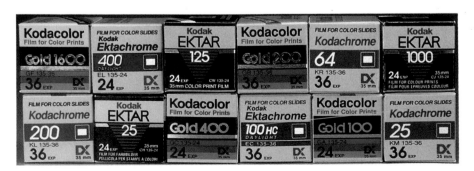

There are other considerations, too. Sharp pictures of action require fast shutter speeds (see the "Exposure" section, pages 138 to 141).

On the other hand, there's a good reason for choosing a slower, less sensitive film. With careful examination, prints or slides from high-speed films don't appear quite as sharp as those from the slower films. This is especially so with enlargements. For scenic pictures, you may decide that it's important to have as sharp an image as possible—from a film with a speed of ISO 25, perhaps.

Choosing a film speed is often a function of what's most important—extreme speed or extreme sharpness. If you don't need the extremes, stick to one of the medium-speed films, ISO 64 to ISO 200, which will be very sharp and still allow you enough speed for moderately fast action or a fairly wide range of lighting conditions.

COLOR BALANCE
Most films give natural-appearing colors in daylight or with flash. Some negative films respond almost as well as tungsten or fluorescent light. If you want correct color rendition in lighting other than daylight, choose a film balanced for a particular light source, or use color-correction filters. (See page 169.)

Daylight—daylight film

Daylight—tungsten film

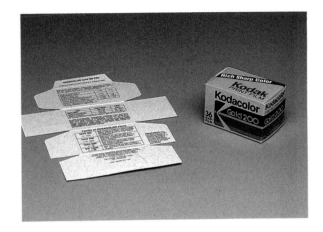

"When all else fails, read the instructions." Actually, the film data inside the box or on a sheet can be very helpful if your meter quits. Some of the information may prove to be valuable casual reading.

FILM INSTRUCTIONS
Some of the handiest information around is in the instructions packaged with some films for automatic and adjustable cameras. You'll find data on exposure, flash, and filters. If your exposure meter quits, read the camera manual. If you are puzzled about filtration, see the inside of the film box.

CARE
All film has a useful life. Usually there's an expiration date printed on the film box. Take pictures and have the film processed before that date.

Extremes in humidity and temperature are film's worst enemies. In heat and high humidity, protect your film and camera as well as you can. For instance, don't store them in the attic or basement. Don't leave them in direct sunlight, the glove compartment of your car, or a similar high-temperature environment. When taking pictures in cold, dry air, keep your camera and film close to your body so that cold film won't get brittle and snap when it is advanced or rewound. Keeping your camera warm will also help prevent static electricity marks on your film.

Try to change film in the shade, even if it's the shade of your own body, to help eliminate fog marks on your film from direct, bright sunlight.

EXPOSURE

Although automatic cameras successfully choose exposure settings without human help, understanding the rudiments of exposure can improve your picture-taking. There are four factors—scene brightness, film sensitivity, shutter speed, and aperture.

Extremely dim light. High-speed film (ISO 400 to 1600) would be a must in this case.

SCENE BRIGHTNESS
Scene brightness can vary widely, from a sunny day at a beach with white sand to a somber plaza lighted only by a shaded street light. To record these extremes and all the variations in between, your equipment must be flexible.

FILM SENSITIVITY
As discussed on pages 133 and 134, film comes in a wide range of sensitivities, or speeds, for a wide range of lighting conditions and applications. Film speed helps determine camera exposure settings. Once you match the film to the situation, an ISO 125 film for fair weather for instance, then you or the camera must adjust the shutter speed and aperture.

Bright light. A low- or medium-speed film (ISO 25 to 200) would work well here.

SHUTTER SPEED

The shutter speed controls the *length of time* that the shutter stays open. The longer the shutter is open, the more light it lets in. When open, it's usually for a very brief time, anywhere from 1/1000 second to 1/30 second. You can see the different speeds on your camera's shutter speed control: 1000 (1/1000), 500, 250, 125, 60, 30, and sometimes 15, 8, 4, 2 (1/2), and 1 second. The B setting is used to make time exposures. Each shutter speed is roughly half or double its immediate neighbor. The shutter will let in half as much light at 1/125 as it will at 1/60 second, but twice as much as if set at 1/250. (Older cameras may have slightly different shutter speeds, such as 500, 200, 100, 50, 25, 15, 10, 5, 2, 1. There's no cause for concern. Operation is exactly the same as with newer values. It might be helpful, however, to have the shutter speeds on an older camera checked for accuracy.)

APERTURE

The aperture controls the *brightness* of light you let into the camera. The aperture on most automatic cameras is adjustable from a large opening, $f/2.8$, to a small opening, $f/22$. Contrary to what you'd expect, the *smaller the number, the bigger the aperture*. The f-number represents a ratio between the size of the aperture and the focal length of the lens. $F/11$ would mean that the aperture diameter is 1/11 the focal length of the lens. Customary aperture numbers are $f/22$, $f/16$, $f/11$, $f/8$, $f/5.6$, $f/4$, $f/2.8$, $f/2$ and occasionally $f/1.8$, $f/1.7$, or $f/1.4$.

Changing the aperture or the shutter speed will change the amount of light that reaches the film. Automatic cameras will compensate for the gain or loss in light. The picture series at right shows the effect of one-stop changes in the aperture setting. Changing the shutter speed would have produced the same results. Most people would consider the image at lower left to be correctly exposed.

Shutter speed dial

Aperture ring

SHUTTER SPEED PLUS APERTURE

The *f*-numbers work in one sense the same way as shutter speeds. An aperture set at *f*/2.8 lets in twice as much light as its neighbor on the scale, *f*/4, but only half as much as its neighbor on the other side, *f*/2. The big surprise is that the unit spacing for shutter speeds and *f*-numbers is comparable. A change from one shutter speed to the next gives the same exposure result as changing from one *f*-number to the next. This means that several different combinations of *f*-number and shutter speed will give good exposure under the same lighting conditions with the same film. For instance, if you set aperture and shutter speed at *f*/8 and 1/125, respectively, you can get the same exposure as if you had set *f*/5.6 and 1/250, *f*/4 and 1/500, *f*/2.8 and 1/1000, *f*/11 and 1/60, *f*/16 and 1/30, or *f*/22 and 1/15-second.

Fast shutter speed

Slow shutter speed

Large aperture

Small aperture

What's the reason for all the numbers? If you think back a second, you'll realize that you need the extensive adjustments to cope with all the possibilities in lighting that you're likely to come across. There are other reasons as well. Fast shutter speeds such as 1/250, 1/500, and 1/1000 will stop rapid action. Slow shutter speeds such as 1/30, 1/15, and 1/8 second are often used intentionally to blur certain action subjects into a swirl of color and motion. Moderate shutter speeds are used for general photography— fast enough to negate hand movement, but slow enough to permit middle-size apertures and medium-speed film.

On the other hand, changing the aperture changes the depth of field (explained in detail on pages 144–145). Large apertures such as $f/2.8$ and $f/2$ give a shallow depth of field where only your subject, or part of your subject, is in sharp focus. Small apertures such as $f/16$ and $f/22$ give great depth of field. Experienced photographers use all these controls— film speed, shutter speed, and aperture size—to keep as much control over the resulting picture as possible.

Exposure Meters. Getting the right exposure for a given situation is often a matter of opinion. Some photographers prefer their photos a little darker than others. Generally, though, acceptable exposure will still show some detail in the brightest areas and some in the darkest.

Most people use manually adjustable cameras with built-in exposure meters or automatic cameras in which a built-in meter sets the shutter speed, the aperture, or both. In any case, the meter will gather the exposure information for you. Always take a reading very close to the subject before stepping back and composing the picture. Check your camera or exposure meter instruction manual for information on its operation.

There are times when a camera exposure meter will not make the right exposure decision. What you must do is recognize the situation and compensate. Here are typical situations and compensations:

Sidelighted subject	increase exposure ½ stop
Backlighted subject	increase exposure 1 stop
Small, bright subject against dark background	decrease exposure 1 stop
Small, dark subject against bright background	increase exposure 1 stop
Average subject in extremely bright scene, such as snow or sand	increase exposure 1 stop

Although camera exposure meters take much of the work out of determining and setting exposure, they often miss in the situations described at left. With an adjustable camera that has a built-in meter, make your meter reading, and then adjust it as recommended at left.

Many automatic cameras offer a way to override manually the automatic exposure feature. It may be a dial that offers up to a two-stop increase or decrease in exposure. There may also be a way to switch the camera to completely manual operation.

Other cameras are entirely automatic with no way to alter the camera-selected settings. If your camera has a film-speed selector, you can alter it to adjust automatic exposure. To increase the exposure by one stop, set the film-speed indicator to a value half of the speed of the film you're using. To increase exposure by two stops, cut the film speed to one quarter of the real value of the film in the camera. The reverse is true for decreasing exposure. Double the film-speed setting for a one-stop decrease in exposure and quadruple it for a two-stop decrease. *DO NOT FORGET TO RETURN THE FILM-SPEED SETTING TO THE CORRECT VALUE AFTER YOU'VE MADE YOUR SPECIAL-SITUATION PICTURE.*

Meter recommendation

Decrease exposure one stop

Meter recommendation

Increase exposure one stop

Exposure Summary.

1. Use medium-speed film in normal outdoor situations, high- or very high-speed film in dim scenes, and low-speed film for the sharpest pictures possible.
2. Use a shutter speed at least as fast as 1/125 second for most situations to prevent camera movement from blurring your picture.
3. Fast shutter speeds capture action; slow shutter speeds blur action.
4. Large apertures give shallow depth of field; small apertures give great depth of field.
5. Usually several combinations of shutter speed and aperture will give correct exposure. Review the reasons for choosing shutter speeds and apertures.
6. Check the manual for your exposure meter or automatic camera to compensate for very bright and very dark subjects.
7. Sidelighting and backlighting often require more exposure than frontlighting—one half and one stop, respectively.

Note: If the film speed selector on your camera cannot register a very high-speed film, such as ISO 1600, compensate by setting it to the highest ISO possible and compensate by using a faster shutter speed or smaller aperture.

DEPTH OF FIELD

Shallow depth of field—f/2   *Great depth of field—f/22*

When you focus your camera lens on a subject, you are unknowingly including a greater area in focus. Each aperture setting gives a different depth of field—that is, the distance range that is in acceptably sharp focus. Small apertures, such as $f/11$, $f/16$, and $f/22$, give the greatest depth of field, while large apertures, such as $f/2.8$, $f/2$, and $f/1.4$, give very little depth of field.

Many single-lens-reflex cameras incorporate a previewer that shows how much of the scene is sharp at different apertures. Other cameras usually include a depth-of-field scale that surrounds the distance scale on the lens barrel. By looking at the indicators for the f/numbers you are using, you can see how much of the scene will be sharp in front of and behind the subject.

Depth of field also depends on the camera-to-subject distance. With the same aperture, depth of field will be shallower if you focus on a nearby object than if you focus on a distant one.

You can include more foreground than background by focusing closer than your main subject but still keeping the subject within the depth of field. The reverse is also true.

You can use your understanding of depth of field to preset your camera in a fast-action situation so that you won't have to refocus as the activity gets close and then recedes. Set the smallest aperture your shutter speed will allow and then focus on the spot where most of the action will take place. Even if things drift back and forth a little, your pictures will still be in focus.

By aligning the indicators for the aperture setting (f-number) on the depth-of-field scale with the distances on the focusing ring, you can see the range that will be in sharp focus. The aperture above is f/11. The indicators—between 16 and 8 on the depth-of-field scale—show that anything at a distance between 7 and 15 feet from the camera will be in acceptably sharp focus.

With a small aperture and preset focus, you can concentrate on the action.

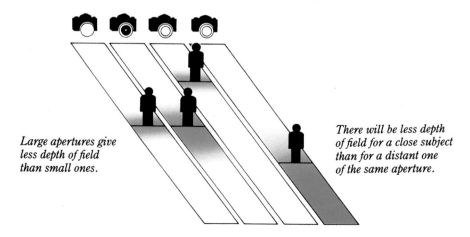

Large apertures give less depth of field than small ones.

There will be less depth of field for a close subject than for a distant one of the same aperture.

LIGHTING

Light is the basis for all picture-taking. Light in the morning is a striking change from light at noon. Bright days are vastly different from cloudy days. Shady spots, open fields, and home interiors, summer, fall, winter, and spring all have their unique light properties—all somehow adaptable for good pictures. Let's first discuss the angles of light that apply for almost any situation.

Frontlighting

ANGLES OF LIGHT

There are three basic lighting angles—frontlighting, sidelighting, and backlighting. Frontlighting means that light is coming from behind the photographer, brightening the side of the subject facing the photographer. A sidelighted subject has light striking one side, and backlighting illuminates the side of the subject away from the photographer. Frontlighting is common for most picture-taking, but it may not give the most effective photos. People tend to squint

Sidelighting

when looking into the sun and dark shadows surround their eyes. Frontlighting is also flat, giving few shadows that help create a feeling of perspective.

Sidelighting is more dramatic, with shadows streaking across the picture, helping to establish shape and three-dimensionality. Sidelighting can also give portraits increased impact. Many photographers prefer backlighting for close-up pictures of people, because their subjects never have to look near the sun. Expressions are relaxed and natural, and there are no contrasting shadow and lighted areas. Backlighting may also give striking scenic pictures, especially early or late in the day, with long shadows racing back toward the camera from rich, black silhouettes. Sidelighting and backlighting require exposure adjustments for properly exposed subjects (not silhouettes). See pages 142-143 in "Exposure" for more information.

Backlighting

IN THE SUN OR OUT

You also have a choice between photographing a subject in bright sunlight or in shade. It depends on the subject. If you want hard, black shadows, photograph in sunlight. If you want a softer quality of light (although a little cooler-colored) take your subject into a shady spot that's clear overhead. There will be plenty of light, but no harshness.

Light, overcast days are excellent for some picture-taking. If you have diffused sunlight that creates soft shadows, you have perfect lighting for a portrait.

COPING WITH SUNLIGHT

Sunlight gives shadows. You can reduce the intensity of these shadows by using a crinkled foil or white reflector to bounce light back at the subject. Experiment by angling a white or foil-covered piece of cardboard in different directions to see how much reflection you want.

You can also use light from a flash device to fill in shadows. (See page 160 in "Flash" for more information.)

DIFFERENT TIMES OF DAY

The color and intensity of sunlight changes throughout the day. Early morning photographers (dawn to 9 a.m.) are rewarded with a soft, pale, sometimes rosy light, painting long shadows that are freshened

Bright sun

Overcast

Dawn

9 AM

Noon

by dew. It's beautiful light for landscapes, especially if you find a few patches of low-lying ground fog. People benefit from this light, too. From 10 a.m. to 4 p.m., sunlight is brilliant and harsh, dropping small, dense shadows. Ordinarily it's not very attractive unless that's the mood you want. From 4 p.m. to sunset, the light deepens in warm tones and lavishly smooths rich shadows across the land. It's dramatic lighting for sidelighted landscapes and sometimes even people. Between sunset and complete darkness comes perfect lighting and color for existing-light cityscapes. (See pages 162-165.)

Without reflector

Bedsheet reflector

INTENSITY
Although our eyes don't see it, there's a vast difference in the intensity of light as it changes. A shaded spot is much darker than a sunlighted area, as is any scene on a cloudy day. Indoors, it's *much* darker than outdoors. (See page 165 in "Existing Light" for more information.) Make sure that you or your camera make the adjustments necessary for changing lighting conditions. (See pages 136-143, "Exposure," and page 133, "Film," for more information about scene brightness.)

Light gives our pictures a chance to appear. It is endlessly variable, and if you study its effects, you'll be able to apply your knowledge to making better pictures in any situation.

With reflector

4 PM

Sunset

SEASONS

As the seasons change, so does the nature of light. Have you ever noticed how much stronger midsummer light is than spring or winter light? Remember those crisp autumn days when the edges of every leaf seem to snap out toward you? Indeed, the lighting is different. Winter with snow finds the sun at a low angle casting weak shadows, reflecting off snow and ice everywhere. Your meter may be fooled by all the whiteness into recommending underexposure. For snow scenes, increase your exposure one stop (see page 142 in "Exposure") over the meter reading. Springtime also brings weakened sunlight, not reinforced by snow reflections. It's beautiful light for people and other subjects not flattered by strong contrast between shadow and light areas. The sun in summer seems to beat down with a vengeance, almost too strong for most picture-taking. By carefully watching the angles and time of day, you can take endless, excellent pictures in summertime, when all the world comes out to play. Clear, strong (but not overpowering) sunlight characterizes autumn. Brilliant for landscapes, it can also give lovely shade-lighted portraits.

Spring

Summer

Fall

Winter

FLASH

When it's too dark to take pictures, the logical decision is to use flash. Some cameras even tell you when it's necessary. There is nothing tricky about flash photography, provided you know the basics and understand your equipment.

GENERAL TIPS

Reflections. Watch out for reflective backgrounds or eyeglasses in the scene. If you take a flash picture directly at either, you'll get an unattractive glare spot in your picture. Stand at an angle to mirrors, windows, or shiny paneling. Ask subjects wearing glasses to turn their heads slightly or remove their glasses.

Reflection in glass

Red Reflections. Some people's eyes (and some pets') can reflect flash with an eerie, often red glow. To avoid red eyes, turn on all the room lights—the extra brightness will help reduce the size of the pupils. Then, if possible, increase the distance between the flash and the camera lens. Some cameras will

Change position

Overexposed foreground   *Foreground objects removed*

accept a flash extender. Finally, back off to a point within the flash range where the reflections will be less noticeable.

Flash Range. With snapshot cameras, photograph subjects within the flash range recommended for your camera, flash type, and film. With other cameras, the range for good flash exposure is determined by the film speed, the aperture setting, and possibly the flash mode.

Overexposed Foreground. Any person or object closer than the near limit of the flash range will be overexposed and too light in your flash picture. Compose the scene so that the main subject is closer than anything else, but still within the flash range.

Subjects scattered at different distances

Several Subjects. Subjects at different distances from the camera will receive different amounts of light—some will be too light or too dark. Make sure that all your subjects are roughly the same distance from the flash.

Subjects grouped at same distance

153

SNAPSHOT CAMERAS

To get well-exposed pictures with your snapshot camera, keep your subject in the correct flash distance range, use fresh batteries, and keep the camera-battery contacts clean. With flashcubes, magicubes, or flipflash, check to see that an unused bulb is in position before making an exposure. If you have an add-on or built-in electronic flash unit, see the general information below.

ELECTRONIC FLASH

The most popular flash accessory for 35 mm cameras is the electronic flash unit. Different systems are detailed in the following pages. Before searching your flash and camera combination, read the general tips below.

1.

1. On a camera with built-in flash, make sure that the film-speed setting is correct for good exposure. Set your film speed on a separate flash unit.

2. If necessary, set the shutter speed recommended by your camera manual for electronic flash. Because the flash duration is typically 1/1000 or less, shutter speed does not affect exposure. If set too fast, however, you'll get partly exposed pictures with a focal-plane shutter or underexposed pictures with a leaf shutter.

2.

3.

3. Focus carefully. Camera-to-subject distance determines exposure with built-in flash.

4. Cameras that don't have built-in flash have an accessory shoe that may be electronically sensitive—a hot shoe. Slide a flash unit with a matching hot foot into the shoe to make the necessary connection. Older cameras or flash units may not be hot. Plug the cord (PC cord), that usually comes with the flash unit, into the flash and camera. If there is a choice of camera sockets, choose the one marked X—the other is for flashbulbs.

4.

4.

5. Flash units take a few seconds to get ready (recycle) for the next picture. The ready light will glow when the flash is ready. When the ready light takes a long time to glow, change the batteries or recharge the flash unit.

5.

BUILT-IN AND ACCESSORY DEDICATED FLASH UNITS

Some 35 mm cameras have a built-in dedicated flash unit or can be matched with a dedicated accessory flash. With a modern dedicated flash unit, you have only to turn on the flash (or camera), focus, and take a picture. The camera and flash make all the exposure settings automatically. Some older dedicated flash units may require you to set the film speed on the flash and to set the aperture on the lens. Because they use circuitry compatible with a specific camera, accessory dedicated flash units will work only with a specific camera brand and often a specific model.

Press a button to raise and activate the flash.

AUTOMATIC FLASH UNITS

Automatic flash units designed to work with any camera are governed by light sensors. When you set the film speed on the flash and select an aperture and a corresponding flash mode, the sensor will govern how much light the flash emits by measuring the intensity of light reflected by the subject. For each aperture and mode combination, the sensor will be able to control flash output over a certain distance range. Read the instruction manual carefully for correct operation of sensor-controlled automatic flash units.

The sensor inside the circle governs flash output.

With an automatic flash unit, you decide what distance range you'll need, choose the appropriate flash mode, and set the aperture. The flash will do the rest to give good exposure. Make sure you set the film speed on the flash unit. The unit pictured is set at its yellow mode which gives a range of 1.6 to 8.5 feet with an ISO 100 film at f/8.

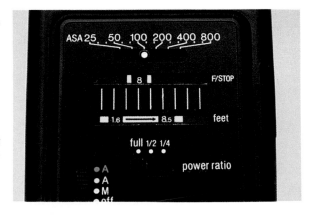

MANUAL FLASH UNITS, MANUAL OR AUTOMATIC CAMERAS

Older or inexpensive flash units operate at full power for every picture. You have to adjust the camera for correctly exposed flash pictures. Since the shutter speed will always be the same (as recommended by the camera manual—usually 1/30, 1/60, or 1/125 second)—you have to set the aperture. Here's a typical operation given in a step-by-step sequence.

1.

2.

1. Attach the flash unit to the camera. If the camera does not have a hot shoe, connect the camera and the flash with a PC connecting cord.*
2. Set the ISO speed of the film you're using on the calculator of the flash unit.
3. Set the correct flash shutter speed on the camera.
4. Turn on the flash unit.
5. Focus on your subject.
6. Check the lens distance scale for the distance between flash and subject, assuming that the flash is attached to the camera. (Exposure is always based on the distance between *flash* and *subject*— not camera and subject.)
7. Apply the distance to the flash unit calculator to find the correct aperture.
8. Set the aperture on the camera.
9. Take the picture.

3.

4.

The process usually takes only a few seconds. Many people preset their cameras at 10 feet, particularly at parties, and take pictures from that distance only.

5.

*Older cameras may require you to choose a socket for the PC cord or select a synchronization setting. If faced with a choice of sockets, plug the cord into the socket marked X for electronic flash. The other socket is for a flash-bulb unit. Set the synchronizing switch at X, as well. Check your camera manual for additional flash-synchronization instructions.

6. and 7.

Note: If the film-speed dial won't register the 1000- or 1600-speed film you're using, set it to 500 and select a lens opening one or two stops smaller than indicated.

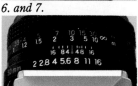
8.

GUIDE NUMBERS

The proliferation of automatic flash systems has nearly erased the memory of a formula used to calculate aperture settings for flash pictures. It may be handy in a pinch.

It works like this. If you know the guide number for your flash unit/film combination, you can easily set the aperture when you know the flash-subject distance. Merely divide the guide number by the distance—the resulting number is the aperture, or very close to it. See the example below.

Guide Number Formula. The guide number of the flash unit is 65 with ISO 100 film. Flash-to-subject distance is 8 feet.

$$65 \div 8 = f/8 \text{ (round when necessary)}$$

Often the guide number for a particular unit is given for only one film speed. Do the same calculations but add or subtract f-stops as indicated by the decrease or increase of speed in the film you're using. (If you're using ISO 100 film and switch to ISO 200 film, perform your usual guide number calculation and then select the next smaller f-stop.)

If you need the guide number for a flash unit that has an exposure calculator, set the film speed, and read the guide number across from the 10-foot distance indicator. The guide number changes for different film speeds.

CARE AND HANDLING

An electronic flash unit's worst enemies are weak batteries and infrequency of use, particularly with rechargeable models that use nickel-cadmium cells. Try to take a few flash pictures every month. Better yet, remove and store batteries in the freezer to preserve their life and protect the flash unit's contacts. Remove the batteries with the power on and the capacitor fully charged to protect the flash unit during storage. Before taking pictures after storage, allow frozen batteries several hours of thawing time to reach room temperature. Then, put them in the unit and form the capacitor by firing the flash manually several times. Remember that weak batteries can shorten the life of your flash unit. It should enjoy a long life.

Replace batteries as recommended. Extend their useful life by occasionally cleaning the contacts with a pencil eraser.

FLASH OFF CAMERA

Moving the flash off the camera flatters many subjects. The lighting gives enough shadow for a three-dimensional appearance.

Removing the flash from the camera may defeat the automatic function of a dedicated flash system. If so, determine exposure by using the manual method described on page 156. Most sensor-operated auto-

Flash on camera

matic units will perform if the sensor is aimed at the subject, and certainly most manual units will work. All you need is an extension PC cord to connect camera and flash. Remember that *flash-to-subject distance* determines aperture setting. It won't be very different if you hold the unit at arm's length. But if a friend or family member holds the flash unit at a distance different from the camera-subject distance, make your exposure adjustments based on the *flash-to-subject* distance.

Flash off camera

BOUNCE FLASH

You can bounce the flash off the ceiling or a nearby wall to improve your subject's appearance. The indirect light is softer, less harsh, and often the soft shadows can help create a feeling of three-dimensional form.

Some sensor-governed automatic units will work correctly, provided that the sensor is aimed at your subject. If this is impossible, operate the unit manually, as you will have to do with some dedicated automatic flash units or a manual unit. Here's how.

Direct flash

Choose a location near a white or light-neutral colored wall or ceiling. The wall may be preferable because it won't cast shadows under a person's eyes. Calculate the distance that the light must travel from flash-to-wall-to-subject. Estimate the aperture necessary for that distance and then open up the aperture an additional two f-stops. For instance, let's say that the distance is 15 feet (7 feet from flash to wall and 8 feet back to the subject) and your flash calculator recommends an aperture of $f/5.6$. Instead of $f/5.6$, set $f/2.8$ on the aperture ring.

Bounce flash

Your wall and ceiling situations are unique. It's a wise idea to experiment a little with slide film and keep records to fine tune your exposure. If you want prints, use a high-speed color negative film during actual shooting, such as KODACOLOR GOLD 1600 Film, to obtain greater shooting distances and smaller apertures.

FILL-IN FLASH

One way to reduce the contrast of shadow and lighted areas in bright sunlight is to fill the shadows with light from an electronic flash. (The results may also be satisfactory with a snapshot camera. Try it and see.) Since you'll be using a fairly slow-shutter speed in bright light, use a low- or medium-speed film so you can set a moderate aperture. KODACOLOR GOLD 100 and EKTAR 125 Films work well.

Manual and Automatic Units. You can add light to shadows in frontlighting, sidelighting, back-lighting, or even in the shade. Too much fill light may make your picture appear artificial. Follow these guidelines for most manual and automatic flash units.
1. Set the shutter speed recommended for flash pho-tography, typically 1/60 second. Set the aperture for the prevailing lighting conditions with that shutter speed.
2. Set the calculator on your flash unit to an ISO number two times the speed of the film you're using so that the flash will not overpower the existing-light conditions.
3. Position yourself and your subject at the distance recommended on the flash calculator for the aper-ture already set on the camera.
4. Expose a flash picture.

Dedicated Units. A SLR camera with built-in flash may have a flash-fill mode you can set (see your camera manual). On snapshot cameras with built-in flash units, just extend the flash and take a picture. There isn't much you can control. Try taping a layer of white tissue over the flash to soften the light. Because operation for dedicated fill-flash varies with different cameras, read the instructions for your outfit carefully. Make sure you don't cover the sen-sor with tissue.

With some KODAK Cameras, you can use the "fill-flash" feature. This prevents underexposure of the main subject caused by a bright, surrounding area that fools the camera sensor.

Flash is a useful tool that will serve you in many more ways than merely brightening dark interiors. Fill-in flash will brighten the shaded side of a subject outdoors, which allows people to look away from the sun.

They can relax their faces and eyes from squinting and offer more cheerful, natural expressions. Flash can also stop fast action for a picture, as in the case of the swinging child above.

ACTION

The duration of electronic flash is usually much shorter than your fastest shutter speed. This high-speed capability can stop even very fast action in dark places—children playing, pets jumping, ping-pong players smashing, and so on. Exposure is based on flash-to-subject distance. Remember that bounce flash provides more natural light.

EXISTING LIGHT

Taking pictures by existing light means picture-taking in dim light without flash. You need a high- or very high-speed film (ISO 400 to ISO 1600) and a lens with an $f/2.8$ maximum aperture or larger. Read the following pointers and have a look at the exposure suggestions on page 165.

Take exposure-meter readings as close to your subject as possible. Avoid reading parts of the scene that include a bright light source, such as this candle. The small spot of bright light may confuse your exposure meter into recommending underexposure.

SOME POINTERS

1. Don't include a bright light source when making a meter reading. The light may fool your meter into recommending underexposure.
2. Make meter readings close to your subject.
3. With an automatic camera, get as close as possible to your subject to take the picture.
4. The side of your subject facing the light should probably be the one you photograph.
5. Since your shutter speeds may be fairly slow—e.g., 1/30 second—hold your camera steady.
6. If you use a shutter speed slower than 1/30 second, brace your camera against something solid or mount it on a tripod.
7. Match your film to the scene lighting. Using filters reduces the light that reaches the film.

8. KODAK EKTACHROME Films can be push-processed one additional stop by your photofinisher. If you're using an ISO 400 film, set the film-speed dial at ISO 800 and expose the whole roll at the same film speed. Then ask for special (push) processing.
9. A wide range of exposures may be acceptable in many existing-light situations. Experiment with different exposures to see what you prefer.
10. At the very large apertures, you'll be using (f/2.8 or f/2), depth of field is very shallow. (See pages 144 and 145 for more on depth of field.) Be sure to focus carefully.
11. Consult the "Suggested Exposures" table on page 165.

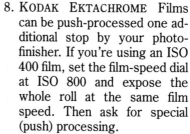

For many existing-light scenes, you can get good photos with a wide range of exposures, as you can see in these views of Niagara Falls. It's wise, in fact, to take several pictures at different exposure settings, so that you'll have several to choose from. Left: 2 seconds at f/4. Top left: 4 seconds at f/4. Top right: 8 seconds at f/4. For this type of scene, you might want to use KODACOLOR GOLD 1600 Film.

Suggested Exposures. Consider the exposure settings shown in the table at the right as guidelines. It's wise to bracket your exposures, especially with slide film, because many existing-light scenes can fool an automatic camera or built-in exposure meter. Typical existing-light subjects may be acceptable over a wide range of exposures, especially outdoors at night.

☐ *For color slides, use tungsten film. You can use daylight film, but your slides will look yellow-red.*

☐ *For color slides, use daylight film or tungsten film with No. 85B filter and 1 stop more exposure.*

☐ *For color slides, use either daylight or tungsten film.*

For color prints, you can use KODACOLOR GOLD Films for all the scenes listed.

In a window-light portrait like this, you'll probably get best results when you take your exposure reading from the bright side of your subject's face. Emphasize that side when you compose the picture.

Suggested Exposures for Existing-Light Pictures

Picture Subject	ISO 64–100*	ISO 125–200	ISO 400‡	ISO 1000	ISO 1600
AT HOME					
Home interiors at night					
Areas with bright light	1/15 sec f/2	1/30 sec f/2	1/30 sec f/2.8	1/30 sec f/4	1/60 sec f/4
Areas with average light	1/4 sec f/2.8	1/15 sec f/2	1/30 sec f/2	1/30 sec f/2.8	1/30 sec f/4
Candlelighted close-ups	1/4 sec f/2	1/8 sec f/2	1/15 sec f/2	1/30 sec f/2	1/30 sec f/2.8
Indoor and outdoor holiday lighting at night, Christmas trees	1 sec f/4	1 sec f/5.6	1/15 sec f/2	1/30 sec f/2	1/30 sec f/2.8
OUTDOORS AT NIGHT					
Brightly lighted downtown street scenes (Wet streets add interesting reflections)	1/30 sec f/2	1/30 sec f/2.8	1/60 sec f/2.8	1/60 sec f/4	1/125 sec f/4
Brightly lighted nightclub or theatre districts—Las Vegas or Times Square	1/30 sec f/2.8	1/30 sec f/4	1/60 sec f/4	1/125 sec f/4	1/125 sec f/5.6
Neon signs and other lighted signs	1/30 sec f/4	1/60 sec f/4	1/125 sec f/4	1/125 sec f/5.6	1/125 sec f/8
Floodlighted buildings, fountains, monuments	1 sec f/4	1/2 sec f/4	1/15 sec f/2	1/30 sec f/2	1/30 sec f/2.8
Skyline—distant view of lighted buildings at night	4 sec f/2.8	1 sec f/2	1 sec f/2.8	1 sec f/4	1 sec f/5.6
Skyline—10 minutes after sunset	1/30 sec f/4	1/60 sec f/4	1/60 sec f/5.6	1/125 sec f/5.6	1/125 sec f/8
Fairs, amusement parks	1/15 sec f/2	1/30 sec f/2	1/30 sec f/2.8	1/60 sec f/2.8	1/60 sec f/4
Fireworks—displays on the ground	1/30 sec f/2.8	1/30 sec f/4	1/60 sec f/4	1/60 sec f/5.6	1/60 sec f/8
Fireworks—aerial displays (Keep shutter open on Bulb for several bursts.)	f/8	f/11	f/16	f/22	f/32
Burning buildings, campfires, bonfires	1/30 sec f/2.8	1/30 sec f/4	1/60 sec f/4	1/125 sec f/4	1/125 sec f/5.6
Night football, baseball, racetracks†	1/30 sec f/2.8	1/60 sec f/2.8	1/125 sec f/2.8	1/250 sec f/2.8	1/250 sec f/4
Niagara Falls					
White lights	15 sec f/5.6	8 sec f/5.6	4 sec f/5.6	4 sec f/8	4 sec f/11
Light-colored lights	30 sec f/5.6	15 sec f/5.6	8 sec f/5.6	4 sec f/5.6	4 sec f/8
Dark colored lights	30 sec f/4	30 sec f/5.6	15 sec f/5.6	8 sec f/5.6	4 sec f/5.6
INDOORS IN PUBLIC PLACES					
Basketball, hockey, bowling	1/30 sec f/2	1/60 sec f/2	1/125 sec f/2	1/125 sec f/2.8	1/250 sec f/2.8
Stage shows					
Average	1/30 sec f/2	1/30 sec f/2.8	1/60 sec f/2.8	1/125 sec f/2.8	1/125 sec f/4
Bright	1/60 sec f/2.8	1/60 sec f/4	1/125 sec f/4	1/250 sec f/4	1/250 sec f/5.6
Circuses					
Floodlighted acts	1/30 sec f/2	1/30 sec f/2.8	1/60 sec f/2.8	1/125 sec f/2.8	1/250 sec f/2.8
Spotlighted acts (carbon-arc)	1/60 sec f/2.8	1/125 sec f/2.8	1/250 sec f/2.8	1/250 sec f/4	1/250 sec f/5.6
Ice shows					
Floodlighted acts	1/30 sec f/2.8	1/60 sec f/2.8	1/125 sec f/2.8	1/250 sec f/2.8	1/250 sec f/4
Spotlighted acts (carbon-arc)	1/60 sec f/2.8	1/125 sec f/2.8	1/250 sec f/2.8	1/250 sec f/4	1/250 sec f/5.6
Interiors with bright fluorescent light	1/30 sec f/2.8	1/30 sec f/4	1/60 sec f/4	1/60 sec f/5.6	1/60 sec f/8
School—stage and auditorium	—	1/15 sec f/2	1/30 sec f/2	1/30 sec f/2.8	1/60 sec f/2.8
Church interiors—tungsten light	1 sec f/5.6	1/15 sec f/2	1/30 sec f/2	1/30 sec f/2.8	1/30 sec f/4
Stained-glass windows, daytime— photographed from inside	Use 3 stops more exposure than for the outdoor lighting conditions.				

*With ISO 25–32 film, increase exposure by 2 stops.
†When lighting is provided by tungsten lamps and you want color slides, use tungsten film
‡You can expose KODAK EKTACHROME 400 Film (Daylight) at ISO 800 when you have the film push-processed. Decrease suggested exposure in this column by one stop.

165

FILTERS

Photographers use filters for a variety of reasons. With color film, filters can enhance or diminish effects of lighting color. They can also correct the color of light for film of a particular balance. (See "Film," page 134.) You can diminish haze and reflections and increase saturation of colors with a polarizing filter. You can use deep color filters, primarily for black-and-white films, for special effects with color film. With black-and-white films, filters can increase contrast, correct tonal relationships, reduce haze, and control reflections.

Many glass-mounted filters are available that will screw directly into the front of your lens.

Other filters are available as acetate squares. The squares fit into special frames.

The frames attach to the front of your lens and can be adapted for a number of lens sizes.

Without polarizer

With polarizer

COLOR FILM

Polarizer. The polarizing filter reduces reflections from airborne moisture in the sky (haze) and from non-metallic sources. This means that sky, grass, and other subjects will show more accurate, richer colors. Aim your camera at a 90-degree angle (approximately) to the rays of light for maximum effect. You may also adjust the effect on most polarizing filters by turning the outer filter ring. A polarizing filter always requires a 1⅓-stop exposure increase. Adjust an automatic camera manually because the meter may not give correct exposure.

Autofocus SLR cameras require circular polarizers; they also work with non-autofocus SLR cameras. Linear polarizers work only with non-autofocus SLR cameras.

Polarizers will reduce reflections from non-metallic surfaces, such as glass and water. You can control how much reflection you eliminate by operating the adjusting ring on the filter. You may want to retain some sparkle in water scenes.

Without polarizer

With polarizer

Color Correction Filters. In the section on "Film," page 134, we discussed films with different color balance. It's convenient if the film in your camera always matches the light where you're photographing. When it doesn't, you can attach the appropriate filter. See the table at right for possible film, light, and filter combinations. Notice also that the table gives exposure adjustments. Since all filters block some of the light entering the camera, you must always give extra exposure. Operate your camera manually if possible. Meter the scene without a filter attached, make the necessary adjustment, and then add the filter for your picture. (This may not be necessary with through-the-lens metering.) One note here—typical household lighting is 2900 to 3200 K tungsten. There are also special lights for photography called photolamps (3400 K), which require a different film and slightly different filters.

Table Instructions

Conversion filters change the color quality of a light source to match the quality of the light for which a color film is balanced. The table at right shows which filter to use with various film and light combinations. The table also shows how much additional exposure to give for the filters listed.

Tungsten light, daylight film, no filter

Add a No. 80A filter for correct color.

Conversion Filters for Kodak Color Films

Kodak Color Films	Balanced for	Filter and f-Stop Change		
		Daylight	**Photolamp (3400 K)**	**Tungsten (3200 K)**
Kodacolor Gold and Ektar Films	Daylight, Electronic Flash	No filter	*No. 80B + 1⅔ stops	*No. 80A + 2 stops
Kodachrome 40 5070 (Type A)	Photolamps (3400 K)	No. 85 + ⅔ stop	No filter	No. 82A + ⅓ stop
Kodachrome 25 (Daylight) Kodachrome 64 (Daylight) Ektachrome 64 (Daylight) Ektachrome 100 (HC/Daylight) Kodachrome 200 (Daylight) Ektachrome 200 (Daylight) Ektachrome 400 (Daylight)	Daylight, Electronic Flash	No filter	No. 80B + 1⅔ stops	No. 80A + 2 stops
Ektachrome 160 (Tungsten)	Tungsten (3200 K)	No. 85B + ⅔ stop	No. 81A + ⅓ stop	No filter

Note: Increase exposure by the amount shown in the table. If your camera has a built-in exposure meter that can make a reading through a filter used over the lens, see your camera manual for instructions on exposure with filters.
*For critical use.

Daylight, tungsten film, no filter

Add a No. 85B filter for correct color.

Fluorescent light, daylight film, no filter   *Add a correction filter.*

When you expose under fluorescent lighting, you'll get best results on color negative film for prints. Use a correction filter on the lens to compensate for the greenish tint from fluorescent lights. These filters are supplied as 3-inch acetate squares. Glass-averaging filters with screw-in mounts are also available. FLD on the filter denotes an averaging filter for fluorescent light with daylight film and FLB or FLT works with tungsten film and fluorescent light.

You can correct color rendition with fluorescent light by using filters over the camera lens.

Left, photo was exposed under fluorescent lighting using daylight-balanced film without a correction filter. Right, photo shows the results with a correction filter.

Open shade, no filter

Add a No. 81A filter.

There are filters that can warm or cool your color picture slightly. Intended for advanced or professional use to get precise matches of film and lighting, they can be very handy for a subject in the blue light of open shade or the fiery light of sunset.

Sunset, no filter

Add a No. 82A filter.

Creative Colors. The filters used for black-and-white photography come in a wealth of rich hues. Sometimes one of these can make a brilliant addition to your color pictures. Naturally, blue filters make your pictures blue, and red filters make them red.

No filter   *Yellow filter*   *Orange filter*

Exposure is a matter of personal preference. Normally it's wise to increase the exposure slightly, but not as much as recommended for correct exposure with that filter and black-and-white films. Experiment a little to see how you like the effects best.

Red filter   *Green filter*   *Deep blue filter*

BLACK-AND-WHITE FILM

Black-and-white film records all colors in many tones of gray—from black through countless grays to white. Subjects that appear nearly white in prints have received a great deal of exposure; dark subjects not nearly as much. Filters transmit their own color of light and subtract others, depending on their color and density. A red flower photographed through a red filter will be nearly white and the green leaves very dark gray.

Exposure. Filters for black-and-white film require exposure compensation. See the table at right for filter and exposure recommendations.

Table Instructions
The table at right shows typical uses for filters with black-and-white film. To apply the exposure information, meter the scene without a filter, make the necessary exposure change, attach the filter, and take the picture.

Color film

Black-and-white film, no filter

Black-and-white film, No. 8 yellow filter

Black-and-white film, No. 25 red filter.

Black-and-white film, No. 25 red filter and polarizer.

Filters can help bring out striking contrasts in black-and-white landscape photos. A No. 8 yellow filter gives the scene a tonal rendition similar to the color version. A red or polarizing filter will heighten the contrast. Adding the red filter to the polarizer makes the scene even more dramatic.

174

Filter Recommendations for Black-and-White Films

Subject	Effect Desired	Suggested Filter	Increase Exposure by:
Blue Sky	Natural	No. 8 Yellow	1 stop
	Darkened	No. 15 Deep Yellow	1⅓ stops
	Spectacular	No. 25 Red	3 stops
	Almost black	No. 29 Deep Red	4 stops
	Night effect	No. 25 Red, plus polarizing screen	4⅓ stops
Marine Scenes When Sky is Blue	Natural	No. 8 Yellow	1 stop
	Water dark	No. 15 Deep Yellow	1⅓ stops
Sunsets	Natural	None or No. 8 Yellow	1 stop
	Increased brilliance	No. 15 Deep Yellow or No. 25 Red	1⅓ stops or 3 stops
Distant Landscapes	Addition of haze for atmospheric effects	No. 47 blue	2⅔ stops
	Very slight addition of haze	None	None
	Natural	No. 8 Yellow	1 stop
	Haze reduction	No. 15 Deep Yellow	1⅓ stops
	Greater haze reduction	No. 25 Red or No. 29 Deep Red	3 or 4 stops
Nearby Foliage	Natural	No. 8 Yellow or No. 11 Yellowish-Green	1 or 2 stops
	Light	No. 58 Green	2⅔ stops
Outdoor Portraits Against Sky	Natural	No. 11 Yellowish-Green No. 8 Yellow, or polarizing screen	2, 1, or 1⅓ stops
Flowers—Blossoms and Foliage	Natural	No. 8 Yellow or No. 11 Yellowish-Green	1 or 2 stops
Red, "Bronze," Orange, and Similar Colors	Lighter to show detail	No. 25 Red	3 stops
Dark Blue, Purple, and Similar Colors	Lighter to show detail	None or No. 47 Blue	None or 2⅔ stops
Foliage Plants	Lighter to show detail	No. 58 Green	2⅔ stops
Architectural Stone, Wood, Fabrics, Sand, Snow, etc. When Sunlit and Under Blue Sky	Natural	No. 8 Yellow	1 stop
	Enhanced texture rendering	No. 15 Deep Yellow or No. 25 Red	1⅓ or 3 stops
Interiors in Tungsten Light	Natural	No. 11 Yellowish-Green	2 stops

Contrast and Separation. One of the main uses for filters in black-and-white photography is to separate subjects of different colors into strikingly different tones. Black-and-white film may see the red tones and the blue tones as nearly equal. A red filter will make the red tones white and the blue tones dark. A blue filter, however, will make the blue tones light and the red tones dark. See the examples at right.

Use color filters to separate tones in black-and-white pictures. In the comparison at right, note the different values given to the red and blue areas by the red and blue filters.

Color correction. Black-and-white film is affected by different qualities of light. Tungsten light is much redder than sunlight. A yellow-green filter can help the film render the correct tonal relationships in a scene lighted by tungsten light.

Polarizer. A polarizing filter will also help reduce haze and reflection in black-and-white pictures while increasing contrast. The guidelines for handling and exposure adjustment are the same as for color film. (See page 167.)

Filters can increase contrast between sky and clouds.

Color film

Black-and-white film, no filter

Black-and-white film, red filter

Black-and-white film, blue filter

LENSES

Single-lens-reflex cameras typically are sold with a normal lens which sees perspective and image size about the same as your naked eye. It is probably a fast lens with an $f/2.8$ or larger maximum aperture. The normal lens is designed for the kind of general picture-taking people do at home, on vacation, and at special events. What about other lenses?

TELEPHOTO LENSES

Telephoto lenses bring subjects closer, making the subjects look bigger and showing less of the scene than a normal lens would. The magnification alters perspective by compressing distance relationships and consequently decreasing depth of field. The strength of a telephoto lens is determined by its focal length—an optical measurement. The normal lens on a 35 mm camera is roughly 50 mm long. A 100 mm lens will give 2X magnification and a 200 mm lens, 4X magnification.

Portrait photographers prefer a moderate telephoto lens (75 to 135 mm with a 35 mm camera) for a large image at a comfortable distance from the subject. The altered perspective gives a pleasing view of

Telephoto lens

the subject's features and the shallow depth of field makes it easy to blur the background at large apertures. Strong telephoto lenses—200 mm or longer—can help you get closer to sports, wildlife, and other distant subjects.

Camera movement is also magnified by telephoto lenses. Use a fast shutter speed (at least the reciprocal of the focal length, i.e., 1/250 second for a 200 mm lens) and give the camera solid support with a tripod to get sharp pictures.

WIDE-ANGLE LENSES

Wide-angle lenses see more of a scene than normal or telephoto lenses, and subjects will be correspondingly smaller. Compared with a normal, focal-length lens, the distance between near and far objects and the depth of field are extended with a wide-angle lens when the subject distance remains the same.

Situations such as narrow streets and building interiors demand wide-angle lenses. But be careful with

500 mm telephoto lens

200 mm telephoto lens

85 mm telephoto lens

people; the perspective can be distorted with close subjects.

Moderate wide-angle lenses—28 to 35 mm—are so useful that many photographers consider them normal lenses. Very wide-angle lenses—18 to 25 mm—are more extreme and are generally used for special applications or to amplify distortion.

ZOOM LENSES

Zoom lenses offer an economical and convenient alternative to a large assortment of single-focal-length lenses. They come in a wide variety of focal-length ranges and give excellent results. When traveling, a typical zoom lens choice would be a 28 to 85 mm zoom and an 80 to 200 mm zoom. These two lenses plus your fast normal lens for dim light could capture nearly any subject, yet occupy little space in your luggage.

55 mm normal lens

28 mm wide-angle lens

18 mm wide-angle lens

CLOSE-UPS

With many cameras, you can usually find a way to isolate small subjects, such as a single big flower or a tidy group of lesser blossoms. The most economical way is with close-up lenses or filters that screw onto the end of the normal lens. More versatile, but more costly, are macro lenses and macro-zoom lenses. Many beginning photographers use the less expensive close-up lenses initially and buy a macro lens later when their techniques have advanced and when their budget allows it.

Close-up lenses come graded in diopters—typically +1, +2, and +3. The higher the number, the closer you can get, and the bigger your image will be. If you have a camera that has a viewfinder separate from the lens, it might be best to use only one close-up lens, a +2 for instance, so that you get completely familiar with how it works. (As you'll see later, close-up lenses require a little measuring and calculation for accurate results.) A single-lens-reflex camera, however, shows you in the viewfinder almost exactly what will be on the film, so you can use any close-up lens, or even a combination of close-up lenses for the best treatment of your subject.

The viewfinder for any rangefinder camera is adjusted to give you accurate framing (you get what you see) from the minimum focusing distance to infinity. When you use a close-up lens for closer distances, the viewfinder will not show exactly what the film will record. And, since depth of field is so shallow at close focusing distances, you'll want the camera lens to be at the precise distance recommended by the close-up lens instruction sheet or in the table on page 185. To aim your camera from the correct distance, attach a string to the camera with a knot tied at the recommended distance. Extend the string until the knot just touches the subject. Then you're at the right distance. When you hold the string out, make sure the camera lens is pointed directly at the subject. Then drop the string and snap the picture. With practice, this becomes a simple and effective way to make close-ups.

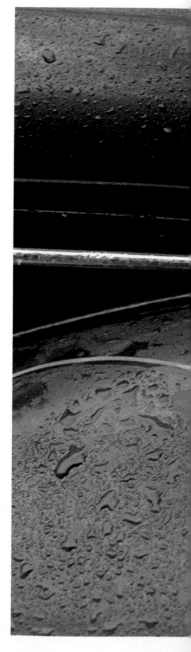

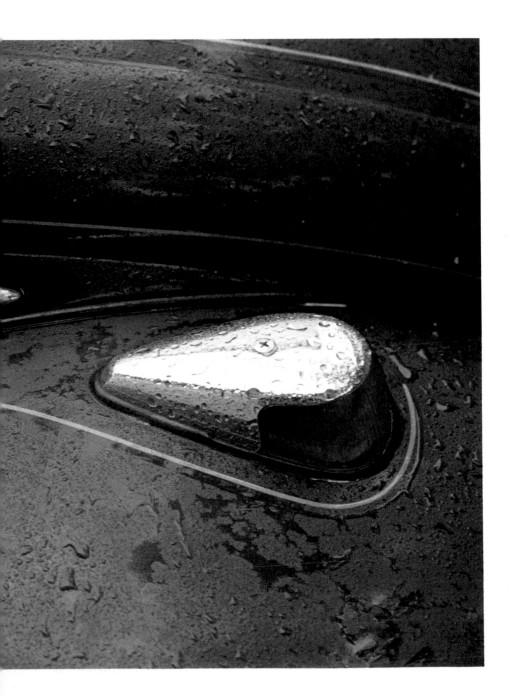

Almost as easy, and much more accurate is a lightweight cardboard measuring device. Cut to the recommended distance, the board should have a lengthwise line at center that you line up from camera lens to subject. The board should be only as wide as the long dimension of the field of view for that close-up lens. That way, you'll know much of the subject will be included in the picture. Make sure the camera isn't tilted up or down, remove the cardboard, and take your picture.

Cardboard measuring device

Shown below is information you'll want to use for taking close-up pictures with a rangefinder camera. The left column shows different close-up lenses and lens combinations at various camera lens focus settings. The next column gives lens-to-subject distances for you to measure. The columns on the right give the field size (subject area) for the combinations shown at left. Just remember to measure the distance carefully from the front rim of your close-up lens to the subject. Aim the camera lens directly at the subject. Incidentally, close-up lenses require no exposure compensation.

Close-Up Lens Data

Close-up Lens and Focus Setting (in feet)		Lens-to-Subject Distance (in inches)	Approximate Field Size (in inches)	
			38–40 mm Lens on a 35 mm Camera	50 mm Lens on a 35 mm Camera
+1	Inf	39	23⅛ x 34½	18 x 27
	15	32¼	18⅞ x 28⅛	14⅝ x 21⅞
	6	25½	14⅝ x 21¾	11⅜ x 16⅞
	3½	20⅜	11½ x 17⅛	8⅞ x 13⅛
+2	Inf	19½	11⅝ x 17¼	9 x 13½
	15	17¾	10⅜ x 15½	8 x 12
	6	15½	8⅞ x 13¼	6⅞ x 10¼
	3½	13⅜	7⅝ x 11⅜	5⅞ x 8¾
+3	Inf	13⅛	7¾ x 11½	6 x 9
	15	12¼	7⅛ x 10⅝	5½ x 8¼
	6	11⅛	6⅜ x 9½	5 x 7⅜
	3½	10	5⅝ x 8½	4⅜ x 6½
+3 plus +1	Inf	9⅞	5¾ x 8⅝	4½ x 6¾
	15	9⅜	5½ x 8⅛	4¼ x 6⅜
	6	8⅝	5 x 7⅜	3⅞ x 5¾
	3½	8	4½ x 6¾	3½ x 5¼
+3 plus +2	Inf	7⅞	4⅝ x 6⅞	3⅝ x 5⅜
	15	7½	4⅜ x 6½	3⅜ x 5⅛
	6	7⅛	4⅛ x 6⅛	3⅛ x 4¾
	3½	6⅝	3¾ x 5⅝	2⅞ x 4⅜
+3 plus +3	Inf	6⅝	3⅞ x 5¾	3 x 4½
	15	6⅜	3¾ x 5½	2⅞ x 4¼
	6	6	3½ x 5⅛	2⅝ x 4
	3½	5⅝	3¼ x 4¾	2½ x 3¾

Attaching + 1 close-up lens

CAMERA CARE

Although your camera is designed for hard use, it is a precision instrument and deserves whatever care you can provide. Here are some guidelines:

1. Protect your camera from dirt and bumps with a case.
2. Keep the inside clean by using a soft brush or air syringe when you load or unload it. You can also use canned compressed air, but follow instructions on the can or in your camera manual carefully. Misuse could damage your camera. Also, aim the air stream precisely—it's possible to blow debris *into* the camera.
3. Keep the lens protected from dirt and fingerprints with a lens cap.
4. Clean the lens by first brushing or blowing off surface debris. Then use photographic lens tissue (not the kind for eyeglasses) and a drop or two of lens-cleaning fluid to wipe off smudges.

1. Use a camera case.

2. Keep the camera clean.

3. Protect the lens.

4. Clean the lens.

5. Shield your camera.

6. Change the batteries.

7. Remove for storing.

5. Protect your camera from water—particularly salt spray—by placing it in a plastic bag or zippered camera case. Attach a UV filter to the lens to protect the vulnerable glass surface from water, dust, sand, and other airborne particles.
6. Change the batteries for meter, flash, and motorized film advance according to the camera manual.
7. Remove the batteries when you store your camera. If left for long periods, they could corrode the camera electrical contacts.
8. Allow a camera used in cold air to warm up gradually when you take it indoors to help prevent condensation. Keep the lens cap attached.
9. Do not leave your camera in a very warm place, such as the glove compartment of your car. Avoid damp basements, too.
10. At the first sign of malfunction, have your camera checked by a competent repair technician.

8. Allow slow warm-up.

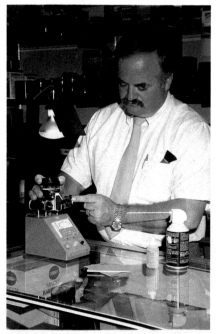

9. Avoid extreme heat.

10. Have a technician check problems.

PHOTO CREDITS

The following list of photographer credits includes comparison, equipment, and technique photos made by Kodak staff photographers and employees. Acknowledgement has been given when the information was available.

Much appreciation is due Kodak Limited, who contributed comparison and technique photos taken in Great Britain and in Europe.

Many of the photographs came from the files of the Kodak International Newspaper Snapshot Contest and the Scholastic Photo Contest. Although many of the entrants are accomplished amateur photographers, a larger number are snapshooters in homes just like yours. The joy and spontaneity of these images should be inspiring and encouraging to picture-takers everywhere.

BIBLIOGRAPHY

KODAK Guide to 35 mm Photography (AC-95)

This book is for the new 35 mm camera owner or for the more advanced photo hobbyist who wants to brush up on the basics. *KODAK Guide to 35 mm Photography* discusses in detail camera handling, Kodak films, exposure, daylight photography, flash, interchangeable lenses, composition, action pictures, existing light, filters, and close-up photography.

Using Your Automatic/Autofocus 35 mm Camera (KW-11)

a KODAK Workshop Series book

Here's a book aimed at providing you with an understanding and working knowledge of automatic cameras and related equipment. It teaches the basics through clear language and pictures.

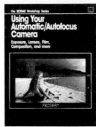

Electronic Flash (KW-12)

a KODAK Workshop Series book

Electronic Flash starts with basics and gives thorough coverage—great advice for the novice and a handy review for someone with experience. Complete technical information plus well-illustrated ideas should give a confident head start in flash photography.

Using Filters (KW-13)

a KODAK Workshop Series book

This book shows you how filters work and how you can use them for color and black-and-white photography. It covers how filters help to reproduce realistic colors and black-and-white tones. Also, there's advice about the creative aspects of filters, complete filter systems, homemade filters, diffusers, accelerators, and far more.

Existing-Light Photography (KW-17)

a KODAK Workshop Series book

This book will introduce you to the exciting world of existing-light photography. You'll learn simple and successful photographic techniques, what films to use and when, and how to set and use your camera in a variety of lighting conditions. It includes conprehensive tables on Kodak films and exposures for existing-light subjects.

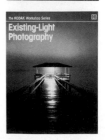

INDEX